Breaking Glass

A Cop's Story of Crime, Terror and PTSD

By Ryan Garland

Author's Note

This book is a work of creative nonfiction: my version of the truth. Dialogue has been reconstructed based on my memories and journals. All names and some identifying details have been altered to protect the individual privacy and anonymity of people whose lives have intersected mine. Some might have different memories or interpretations of the events described in these pages. Their versions, of course, could also be true.

Those who 'abjure' violence can only do so because others are committing violence on their behalf.

— George Orwell, *Notes on Nationalism*

There is no such thing as justice — in or out of court.

— Clarence Darrow

Garland in mask; Nashville Flex Gang Unit 2000

Contents

Preface

Unless someone like you cares a whole awful lot, nothing is going to get better. It's not.

— Dr. Seuss, *The Lorax*

The police academy and Federal Air Marshal Service drilled one lesson into me— vigilance. I learned to see any shift in color, contrast, or motion in an environment as a cue that something is changing and requires my attention. Such changes happen continuously. I want bad things to happen. I thrive in conditions and situations where bad things do happen. I'm needed. I'm wanted. I'm a hero and desire, above all, to be a hero. I watch my surroundings. I watch you not paying attention, and I see the predators watching you.

Pulling into a gas station to fill up and grab a quick coffee? Even in such a mundane situation, I'm on high alert. One day I went to a Mapco, my local convenience store in Nashville, for Tostitos and a six-pack of Budweiser. While perusing the chips in the back corner, I noticed a car pull in and park next to the gas pump farthest from the store. It parked so its gas tank door faced away from the pump. Two men got out and spoke. One looked around while the other walked toward the store.

"Jesus Christ, call 911!" I ordered the clerk. "Tell them you are in a robbery in progress and an off-duty Metro cop is here and say I have on a brown jacket!" He noted my crew cut, watched me draw my gun and clip my badge onto the collar of my jacket, and started dialing for dollars. I moved to the rear of the store and thought about how absolutely surprised this motherfucker was going to be when he entered. Seeking cover, I moved behind a lovely stack of NASCAR Jeff Gordon #24 12-pack Pepsi cases, stacked up pretty high, and waited. As the thug walked in, he reached behind his waist. As he opened his mouth to shout at the clerk, his gaze locked onto mine, I raised my gun and almost got out, "Police!" before he turned and ran like a madman toward his car. If I gave immediate pursuit, I knew I'd be inviting two

thugs to shoot at me when they wanted nothing more than to escape,

so I waited until they were getting into their car. Then I ran out and

grabbed the license plate number as their vehicle screeched out of the

parking lot, turned, and sped toward the intersection fifty feet away,

where five Metro cars were flying into blocking positions.

It seems they'd just robbed another store about two miles

away. There they'd shot the clerk and were seen heading up Harding

Place, a major road with access to I-65, which is good for fleeing. It so

happened they found another Mapco at the intersection. With all the

cops in the area looking for the vehicle, and then the clerk's 911 call, it

hadn't taken more than two minutes for everyone with blue lights to

pack the intersection.

Anyway, that's why I survey the parking lots of gas stations,

rest stops, and convenience stores before I go inside. That' s why I'm

slightly agitated when I pull in and why I might be slightly aggressive

for an hour after I've driven away.

Or how about the call that went out at 17th and West for a

"Robbery in Progress, Silent Alarm," just as I was pulling into the back of the store? The suspect fired two shots in surprise when he saw my car and ran out the front door. I ran inside the store to see if everything was OK as I called in a description of the suspect, but I noticed something strange: very eerily, no one was talking or moving a muscle. The clerk stared straight ahead and four people were in line, still as statues. I got everyone down at gunpoint, deciding to be ready to shoot if some Stephen King shit was going to happen. Turned out, the last guy in line was the second robber and he had a gun in his front sweatshirt pocket. He'd seen his partner in crime fire two shots at my car and run and, not having much of a plan, he'd announced he'd shoot anyone who moved or said anything if a cop came inside.

Stories like those pop up in my mind, fire up my adrenaline, and prepare me for what my mind believes will be an inevitable life-and-death situation. It happens every time I get gas. It happens every time I go to the grocery store. I am always distracted.

My shopping experiences are not the same as yours. You walk through the grocery store parking lot, say "Excuse me!" to a rude driver, hold the door open for a fellow human being, shop, and buy your groceries. I check the store parking lot for threats, looking at people inside vehicles and standing by vehicles. Before exiting my vehicle, I check to see if anyone is coming to block me in, if there are any vans nearby, or if anyone suspicious and out of place is around. As I exit my vehicle, I scan again, looking for movement of color, contrast, or motion that could indicate a threat. I observe those around me to see if anyone has altered course based on the direction in which I begin walking. I look at everyone's hands: are they visible? I look at their clothing: does it match the weather? I watch for clothing bunches near the waist or under the arms, indicating a weapon. If anything changes, I alter my route to see if someone else alters theirs. I observe people in the glass of the store as I approach. I watch vehicles that may be coming toward my position.

Once inside the store, I immediately access the surroundings for danger. I listen and observe the checkout line to determine if any employee is having difficulty with a customer. I proceed down a couple of aisles and note the continued movement of any nearby subjects and to observe if anyone is interacting with anyone else covertly. I then get the peanut butter I came for and proceed to the checkout line, once again checking each individual for indications of danger or hostility. I pay and exit quickly, walking away from my vehicle while observing anyone standing near the exits or near my vehicle. I find and check the cart retrievers in the parking lot to make sure their dress is appropriate to the job. I make sure no one is near me when I enter my vehicle, to be certain I am not purposefully trapped inside.

I exit the parking lot, noting which cars are behind me. I first travel away from my house, switch directions to observe if any countermeasures are being taken, and finally return home. Drained and sad, I put away the peanut butter, images of violence from all the parking lot and grocery store incidents I have endured never leaving my mind.

One evening, while leaving the American Embassy in Tel Aviv, I did not do enough of those things and I was taught a lesson. The other agents and I seemed to have made some people angry at a meeting place near the Diamond District. It was an alley frequented by prostitutes where Hasidic Jews picked up girls, got serviced in their car, dropped off the girls, and drove away. It was a great meeting place in a busy area where people kept their eyes low. That night, while returning from the embassy, I wasn't circuitous and cautious enough and was knocked out cold while crossing a construction site that I thought was open enough to give me a view of anyone approaching.

When I awoke, I was naked. All my clothes were in a neat pile next to me as if Mary Poppins had done the folding. The pile included my wallet and now worthless phone, hidden on the bottom so it wouldn't be stolen. In the dirt someone had drawn two knuckles, an extended middle finger, and two more knuckles: the bird. While humorous in some ways (OK, pretty fucking hysterical), it was scary in others.

I realize I'm not being followed now, but my brain remembers the lesson and fires up, anyway.

Anyone know what a pedophile looks like? I do. You can see them if you look hard in parks, playgrounds, Disney World, and other places kids hang out. I do see them. I'm a predator hunting predators. I want to see one approach a kid so I can destroy him. That's why I'm distracted and not watching the ducks. My adrenaline is going and I'm looking for predators, be they pedophiles or muggers.

I watch like a hawk every time I see a police car on a traffic stop. I slow down and wait until everything looks normal. On some occasions, I have stopped and stood with cops on the side of the road because I knew the situation could turn bad. I could not live with myself if I ever heard of a cop dying on a traffic stop minutes after I

drove away. I want them to be safe; I want to protect them. Part of me

also hopes to God a fight breaks out so I can unleash the rage.

People don't know me as the guy who did some amazing things

trying to protect other people. They don't know me as an expert in

security or an international terrorism investigator. They don't know I

captured a terrorist and made the second page of the *New York Post*.

They just know me as the angry guy with a perverse sense of humor,

the guy with the thousand-yard stare. The guy who's amped up like it's

game day all the time. But they don't see the predators around them,

and I do. I know the predators see me watching them and they look at

me. Sometimes, because of this silent exchange, they don't attack. No

one sees that, either.

Some days, if I'm in an area that's too crowded, a barrage of

flashbacks besiege me and I get lost in the images and pain. My storm

comes: my heart rate escalates, my adrenaline flares, and everything

inside speeds up and feels like it's approaching the red line. The pain,

blackness, and adrenaline stay for hours. At the end, I'm exhausted.

Unable to function, I sleep for hours. Then I'm fine. For a while.

Then there are the nightmares. Before I got the medicine I now take, which is supposed to knock me out at night, I drank myself into a coma to keep the nightmares from destroying the night. Thank God, the meds help. I suck it up, knowing that at least most of the images and occurrences are in the past, and my new roads won't constantly bring more death and violence.

As of this writing, twenty-seven percent of those diagnosed with Chronic Post-Traumatic Stress Disorder have attempted suicide. Dr. Jonathan Shay, a psychiatrist who has worked with combat vets for twenty years, has authored two books about PTSD as a psychological and moral injury. "It's titanic pain that these men live with," he writes. "They don't feel that they can get that across, in part because they feel they deserve it, and in part because they don't feel people will understand it. ...it's despair that rips people apart [who] feel they've become irredeemable."

The Badge of Life, a group of former cops dedicated to preventing police suicide, reports about 145 police officers in the United States take their lives every year, twice the number killed by felons. I can almost guarantee they all have PTSD.

Media reports revealed suicides among active-duty military personnel averaged one per day in 2012.

Life doesn't get much better in the years after service. By the end of 2012, more than three hundred thousand veterans of the Iraq and Afghanistan wars — one in five —were diagnosed with PTSD, according to Face the Facts USA, a project of The George Washington University. By mid-2013, treatment costs for the disorder had reached $2 billion. Veterans now account for 20 percent of suicides in the United States.

They all fought to protect you. I tell my story for them, and so that everyone can understand the personal costs of public service.

Ryan Garland

Upper Saddle River, New Jersey

July 2015

Prologue

Life all comes down to a few moments. This is one of them.

— Bud Fox, Wall Street

January 28, 1998, Nashville

"Unit 542! Shots fired! Shots fired! Start an ambulance! Suspect down! All personnel are 10-4!"

As that sentence tore through the police radio, I stood in a bank parking lot and watched the life leave the bank robber's face. The sergeant walking by me spoke into his radio, "Dispatch, suspect is a Code 4." I had just turned twenty-four years old and I had killed my first person.

Up to that point, it had been an ordinary day. I'd been eating at

McDonald's when a Code 1000PE call was dispatched on the radio.

Code 1000 is a bank robbery. "P" stands for "in progress" and "E" for

"emergency." This one was at the Suntrust Bank at Twenty-first

Avenue South and Edgehill Avenue, right outside the Vanderbilt

campus, at the corner of the Vanderbilt University School of Medicine.

Now, I hadn't been particularly close to this bank robbery: it was

actually way south of my 124 zone. But, having graduated from

Vanderbilt University, I knew the area well and I was certain I could be

of use if someone had seen something. So I ran from McDonald's, hit

the sirens, and made it to the Suntrust four to five minutes after the

call was dispatched. I wasn't the first officer there, so I stayed in my

car in the middle of the street and waited for a vehicle description or

any kind of egress information. I looked up at Hunan Express and the

Pizza Place, two restaurants popular with students, and remembered

all the hours I'd sat on Hunan's balcony eating decent Chinese food

with Eli, Ian, and Grayson, my friends from the Vandy soccer team.

Just eighteen months earlier, as Vanderbilt seniors, we'd sat up

there and talked about our plans for the future. Eli was a Floridian. If

you've ever met a true Floridian, you know Eli. He's as laid back as they come, loves the ocean, and loves to hunt the Everglades. Ian

already had done amazingly well in business and was torn between

joining his dad or grinding his own path. Grayson wanted to move

back to Florida where he could fish and hunt, but he had a girlfriend

with family in Nashville (and you know what that means). Both Eli

and Grayson were engineers, so they would do well wherever. When

you're twenty-two, life seems full of promise. You think you can do

anything.

Me, I would be a lawyer and go into politics. I'd studied

philosophy and ancient Greek/Roman history and almost had a minor

in religion. I'd also just won the Commodore Award, given to the top

student leader of the Vanderbilt Class of 1996. I was president of the

Student Athletic Advisory Board and had made inroads in politics in

Kansas City, where I grew up. I admit my plan was aggressive: I was

going to be a cop for three years, go into the Marines and to Officer

Candidates School, get a law degree, make the rank of captain, and

then come out at thirty-one or thirty-two years old with a fantastic

pedigree for politics. I was going to have a great wife and two kids, go

to church, and have barbecues.

That balcony was a great place from which we could look at the real world without having to participate in it just yet. In the

springtime, we could smell the magnolia trees blooming, sit back, see

the sunset over the Twenty-first and Edgehill intersection, watch the

cars going home during rush hour, and know we weren't too far away

from that reality. Just before anxiety could reach us, we got another

pitcher of beer, talked about the unlimited possibilities of the future,

and, more importantly, of that coming night. We kept reality at arm's

length. Suntrust bank was just another building in the noisy

background. It wasn't even visible from that perch.

Drifting back to reality in my police car, I thought, *Where would
I go if I was a bank robber?* Now that's top-notch police work there;

you can't teach that kind of inspired situational analysis. Just as I was

trying to figure out where to go, the officer who'd arrived first at the

Suntrust, said over the radio, "The bank employees say he ran behind

Hunan Express." I was in front of Hunan Express, so I turned into the

parking lot behind the restaurant, exited my police car, and radioed,

"124, 97 here behind Hunan Express." The next piece of information

came almost instantly from the officer at the bank: "The bank

employees say he has two guns and a hand grenade. One employee

says she sees an officer. She says the suspect is behind a white

[Pontiac] Bonneville."

In front of me, about ten paces, was a white Pontiac Bonneville, parked next to a red Nissan. I radioed, "124, I got the Bonneville." The dispatcher said, "10-4, all cars, close the air for 124 behind Hunan Express with the white Bonneville. All cars, respond to 124 code 3 emergency." I drew my Glock 22 .40-caliber pistol and walked toward the passenger side of the Bonneville. About fifty feet away, another cop was closing in as well. As I reached the trunk, three things happened instantly: Someone yelled, "Gun!" I saw the suspect crouched, hiding behind the car, by the driver's side door, and I saw the orange-red flash as his gun fired at me from five feet away. My brain said, "I'm dead" and it believed that. I waited to feel death. Time slowed. Less than a quarter of a second seemed to take ten seconds. Everything went silent and the world disappeared into blackness everywhere except for the orange-red flame coming to lick my face. Somehow my brain, sure of its own death, got the command "Fire!" to my hands. I watched as my first round struck the suspect without the effect I was looking for. *Maybe he's wearing a bulletproof vest?* Turns out, he was. I fired again. His face ripped open. Then everything sped up to normal, and I could hear again. I heard screaming. I realized I wasn't dead. He had missed. We had fired at each other and he had missed. I walked

toward the suspect, gun drawn, listening to Officer 542 yell into the

radio, "Unit 542! Shots Fired! Start a 47 (Ambulance)! Suspect Down!

All personnel are 10-4!"

I walked to his body and stared as the pool of blood around

him grew into a maroon puddle. I kicked two guns away from him.

Turned out, the hand grenade was fake. The sergeant grabbed me and

led me to his car so I could sit, away from everyone, until the homicide

detectives came.

The song on the radio in the sergeant's car was Bitter Sweet

Symphony by The Verve. I called my mother. "Mom," I said. "I think I

just killed someone, I'm OK, not shot, but I shot someone. He shot first

and I didn't die." Mom threw up. I got off the phone and tears welled in

my eyes. I was trying to figure out how I hadn't died. Eventually, the

Alcohol, Tobacco and Firearms Unit found the round he fired behind

me in a tree. The FBI had wanted the bank robber for netting almost

$1.7 million in eight states. He had stolen $324,000 from the Suntrust

Bank that day.

Hours later, I saw Vanderbilt students interviewed on various

TV news stations. Not surprisingly, they were sitting in Hunan Express and the Pizza Place enjoying a Friday afternoon when the chaos started. They came out to see what was happening. They didn't know they saw a kid playing a game that had just ended, a kid who, eighteen months ago, would have been eating pizza with them. That night, I got home about eleven. I wanted the answer to one question. I stood in the shower, water streaming over my body, tears running down my face, and looked up through blurry eyes.

"Jesus, why?" I asked. "Why? I was almost killed — for what? What was I almost killed for?" I couldn't think of why. I couldn't decipher the puzzle, and I was no longer willing to take the standard cliché answers with which religion placated people. "Dear Jesus, you presume to use my life for your good? I'm on some divine plan? You presume to make me do 'bad' in your name? How can I do things the devil loves in the name of goodness? Why are you destroying me in the name of goodness?"

There was no reply.

I didn't know what to do on the inside—the place where my soul lives, where I cry, where pain in my heart is born. I didn't know what to do about my soul because it was tearing me into two halves —

a boy and a wolf.

Chapter 1:

When You Fight

Monsters

"He who fights with monsters should look to it that he himself does not become a monster. And when you gaze long into an abyss, the abyss also gazes into you."

— Friedrich Wilhelm Nietzsche

January 2000, Nashville

"What do you tell me?" I asked the priest, in a tone too angry and loud for his station. "Is a man who does violent things against another man, things that would make the devil smile and God cringe, a good man?" The confessional booth in which I sat smelled of guilt and candle smoke. The church was made to show power but all I could feel was impotence in the face of my true moral dilemmas: Jesus, who'd been so unable to get down from the cross, was going to help me? The candles in the sanctuary almost brightened from the fuel of the rage within me. The priest wore his uniform of unconditional love and I my uniform of battle, decorated with ribbons for doing violence that had shrunk my soul into little more than a vessel for holding anger and courage. We were at odds, the priest and I, despite both of us doing the "Lord's work," whatever that was. I was doing it like the Archangel Michael, with my sword, while he sheltered himself and thought he could heal me with forgiveness through his words.

"Good men must do heroic things sometimes to achieve God's will," the priest said. "The Bible tells us 'Blessed are the Peacemakers.'"

"Good men don't do bad things, think bad thoughts, and commit violence toward other men. The Peacemakers aren't blessed.

They're damned," I said, exiting the booth and slamming the door

before walking out of the church.

In the year after the shooting, I had entered church after

church in Nashville —Methodist, Presbyterian, Baptist, and this

Catholic Church — to ask the same question. I wanted an answer to my

paradox. All I found were platitudes and forgiveness. I sought neither.

You forgive me? I forgive me, too. But forgiveness didn't answer my

question: how much hate can one man hold inside, and how much

violence can he commit, before he becomes one of the monsters he is

fighting?

I think there's a reason Jesus said, "Love your enemies." Love

contains redemptive power that eventually transforms individuals.

Love builds up: it creates. Hate tears down: it destroys. When you love

your enemies, you transform them with your love.

I don't seek forgiveness because I couldn't love my enemies. At

that point, I didn't even see them as people. After that, of course, I

stopped caring about the people I had sworn to protect. Then I

stopped caring about me. I just hated. My hatred made me strong—

reckless, but strong. Inside, though, buried deep, was a tiny light of hope that no darkness, no evil, no hatred could extinguish.

We each get only one life, as far as we know, and the struggle police officers and soldiers face is predicated on one question: how much is my life worth? Some days mine was worth a twenty-dollar crack rock. Other days, my life was worth nothing. When the world decides not to value your life, but is willing to build memorials to your death, you learn your value is only in your death. So you seek your glory on the line between life and death because that's the only place you feel your value. You morph into something beyond good or evil, something just trying to survive while desperately attempting to recall why surviving is important. Then it's a question of what survives: Me? My soul? The wolf, symbolizing that primal part of every being that lives on animal instincts and concerns itself only with survival and not with morality?" I kept giving up pieces of myself to survive and I became, well, who I am now.

I walked into a lot of churches in Nashville simply to shout at priests and ministers. I wanted them to feel the pain of the paradox of the Peacemaker who is supposedly so blessed. The churches were glorious representations of the "House of God." That's how I thought of them, anyway. I think they want you to be intimidated by God but all I heard, when I walked in, were my own footfalls. It was no different the day I walked into a Methodist church across from Vanderbilt after a horrible car chase and subsequent foot chase. I was still in uniform. To the left was a shrine where people light candles for their prayers. *Ritual*, I thought. *It's what we do when logic fails.* In the front was a stained glass window above an empty cross, signifying Jesus's resurrection, not his death.

That day, I'd been standing in line at a CVS pharmacy near Twenty-first Avenue South at Vanderbilt Avenue and an officer radioed that a vehicle wasn't stopping for him and was heading toward the Edgehill Projects. Realizing it was headed toward me, I ran out of the CVS, slammed on my lights, and boom! Everyone came, screaming, around the corner, lights and sirens blaring. I jumped right in as the second police car.

The suspect tried to lose us in the Project Circle (what we called the U-shaped drive in Edgehill) but swerved into a light pole and careened off the road. The brown buildings were glowing gold in the setting sun. It was a winter sun, the kind that shines right in your face around 4 p.m., making it difficult to see anything when you're driving west. The suspect jumped out and took off, running, though it was clear that his middle-aged druggie frame wasn't going to outrun us up the paved sidewalk hill. I tackled the guy as we were running up the hill. As we hit the ground, he turned on me with a silver object in his hand. The object shone for a quick second in that bright sun and I knew it was metal. He stabbed my chest and I almost screamed in pain, but it wasn't a knife. It was a crack pipe. I rolled over on him and, knocking the pipe from his hand, handcuffed him.

When I walked into that Methodist church, I knew I would have been dead if that ass had had a knife in his hand. I walked in angry and laughing. I was sneering and covered in scrapes from the pavement. Blood from my hands and arms darkened the sleeves of my navy uniform. I hurt inside, so I sneered because I was "the Peacemaker" who was "blessed." I didn't light a single candle. I never did. *Why should I?* I thought. *No one is listening to me.* I laughed at God as I denounced him to the ministers and priests. Their God could live in their houses, I told them, but certainly not on the streets where I worked. When I left, I smashed my fist against their pews. At home, I took off my uniform, threw it against the wall, and drank myself to sleep.

Yet I went into church after church, needing Him to hear me.

Even if he didn't respond ever—and he didn't—I wanted him to know I

was more powerful. I was fighting His fight in His silence. He was the

coward. I was the warrior in the arena. The sun always rose on a new

day and I'd wake up and throw myself into violence again, just to

prove I did more good than their absent God. Part of me wanted so

desperately to be killed on duty, just to stop the pain. I lived in shame

when I saw fellow inner-city cops actually able to live in that darkness.

I also felt shame that I was not killed. If I was killed, I would be valued.

Bagpipes would play "Amazing Grace" at my funeral. People would

weep. There'd be love in my death, though I wouldn't be able to feel

that love. Still, it would be better than this life. I was so very far from

my Kansas roots.

* *

My father was Richard Garland. He grew up in a poor Southern

family in Georgia and Florida. His parents were divorced early and

remarried, each couple having at least one new child of their own. That

made my father the only child between his mom and dad, and, as a

result, he suffered. I don't think Dad felt he received the same love as

his new stepbrother, Donald (the son of his mother, Norma, and his

new stepfather, Walt). Nor, perhaps, did he receive the same love as his new stepsisters, Kathy and Mable (the daughters of his father, Paul,

and his new stepmother, Mary). Dad was passed back and forth, not

really fitting into either family. His mother, Norma was quite a bit

American Indian and a whole lot Southern. His new stepfather, Walt,

was a wonderful man. He was a Seabee in World War II, a sheriff's

deputy at one point, and a Civil War historian. I always admired "Pop,"

as we called Walt, because he had great black hair he slicked back with

a comb and he said, "Hello, Ryan," as if I were an adult. Also, Pop would

play ball with me and buy me toy guns and Michael Jackson magazines.

Dad's real father, Paul, seemed like a great grandpa, but we

weren't allowed to see him very much because he was "a bad

influence." I was not sure what that meant. Nor am I sure now. He gave

me a really cool knife one time, told me to always drink beer from a

bottle, and had some World War II tattoos. Remember the old, green-

looking ones of the 1940s pinups? Yep, those kinds of tattoos.

I never had a connection with any of Dad's side of the family,

except for Pop. Everyone lived too far away and relationships were

always strained. Suffice it to say, I never had grandparents, aunts,

uncles, or cousins who had a real impact on me. I loved them all

because that's what you were supposed to do and we were family. I liked when Norma Nan and Pop would visit in their big, tan

Oldsmobile. Norma was a fierce protector of animals and spoke about

her American Indian ancestors. Pop would indulge her, tell stories of

the Civil War (from the Southern perspective), and smoke cigarettes in

a slow, wistful manner, like he was deep in thought and on the verge of

figuring it all out, if he could just put his finger on a particular word.

Dad wanted to be a psychologist because he liked to

understand human behavior and, probably, because his childhood

wasn't great, and his mom, Norma Nan, was anxiety ridden and a touch

nuts. I think Dad liked psychology the same way my sister always liked

math: they thought that they could find the answer and that the

answer would solve the question. Works in math, not in psychology.

When I was about four years old, Dad would read me *The Hobbit.* I

dearly loved to hear the adventures of Bilbo Baggins. I named all my

stuffed animals "Bilbo" in honor of the brave Hobbit from The Shire.

Dad was a lot like Bilbo — a reluctant adventurer. He was a big

believer in travel as education and thought it was important for my

sister and me to experience new parts of the world and ways of living.

Secretly, though, Dad was a massive worrier. Travel made him very

tense and the stress made him short tempered and anxious. Of course, it probably didn't help that I was a massive risk taker, even early on.

As we all are, Dad is complicated. He is intelligent, thoughtful, scientific, ill tempered, anxious, loyal, critical, and still somehow loves Rush Limbaugh. Dad knows his stuff on almost any subject, too, and you had better have a prepared, well-reasoned point of view if you are going to engage him in a discussion about anything. When it came to parenting, Dad was very analytical and scientific. You did not want to be called into his study and find him behind his desk: that meant it was time for behavior graphs and trouble. My sister and I would have to look at graphs analyzing various good actions and grades and the "opportunity costs" of bad ones. He told us about free will and that we could act in whatever manner we chose, emphasizing that we would never escape the consequences of our actions. A grades = A Privileges and B grades = No privileges. What did I learn? That escaping consequences equals risk taking. The greater the risk taken, the greater the reward, but, if caught, the more dire the consequences. I was taught that consequences matter and that intentions, though nice, often are irrelevant to results.

Judging from the pictures, mugs, statues, and other paraphernalia in Dad's study at home and office at work, he idolized two people —Sherlock Holmes and Don Quixote de La Mancha.

Sherlock Holmes represented Dad's scientific side. He was always intrigued with the mysteries of human behavior and working his mind to solve riddles and help people find solutions to their problems. Don Quixote stood for Dad's romantic side. Dad believes in "eye for an eye" justice. He would take up lance and sword, gather the reins, and sing "Man of La Mancha":

> *And a knight with his banners all bravely unfurled*
> *Now hurls down his gauntlet to thee!*

Of course, he would usually only metaphorically "hurl down his gauntlet to thee." Dad was a very big proponent of standing up for yourself and being fair. However, he wasn't keen on the concept of "the wild winds of fortune" carrying him onward "whithersoever they blow." Remember, he was, if any kind of adventurer, a reluctant one.

The main difference between my dad and me has always been the way we analyze a potential action. Dad's almost sole decision-making parameter is this: "If the consequence of the worst possible outcome of an action is sufferable, only then should the action be taken." Because of whatever natural instinct a male has to overcome his father's rule, and probably because of some genetic and epigenetic wiring, I am somewhere on the other end of the risk spectrum. I

measure the value of the outcome against the failure of the outcome.

Here's my parameter: Is it possible to achieve a certain action that has

value? Then I will probably do it. If an action has value and will bring

glory, I'm doing it, no matter what the consequences—even death.

Let me give you an example. We had a Sea Doo waverunner at

the Lake of the Ozarks, a fifty-mile, man-made lake between Kansas

City and St Louis. I would get behind huge cruisers and jump the Sea

Doo as high as I could make it go. My father, of course, frowned on this

behavior, which didn't pass his test for worthwhile actions. What was

the greatest pleasure to be gained? Yelling "Yeehaw!" and proving to

the world I was a little crazy. What were the potential consequences?

Death, decapitation, or paralysis. Conclusion: the behavior should not

be permitted. Ergo, Ryan can't ride the Sea Doo if he jumps big cruiser

waves. Consequently, I jumped the Sea Doo when Dad wasn't looking. I

could do it, so I did it. There was some conflict between us, but not

much more than that between any father and son—hardly any at all,

really.

When I was young, my favorite game to play with my dad was

"War." We each had a bag of those little, plastic, green Army men and a dart gun that shot rubber darts. We would set up our men around a

base — maybe the fireplace or the coffee table — and take turns trying

to "kill" each other's guys by shooting them with the rubber dart, like

snipers. We'd take out the Army guys, one by one, until a winner was

decided. It was such a fun game as well as an introduction to guns and

strategic thinking at an early age.

Now, I must tell you about "the farm." There was true proof

that long, long ago, in a galaxy far, far away, my father loved my

mother: he purchased the farm. This brings me to Mom who sees

herself, above all else, as a teacher. That's important to understand

because being a teacher, by definition, presupposes knowledge about

whatever you're teaching. Mom does have a master's degree in

education and worked in the field a long time. When we were growing

up, though, she just stayed home with us. So she taught us what she,

from her experience, thought was best.

Mom was raised in Kansas City, Kansas, in the '40s and '50s, so

she missed the hippie culture of the late '50s and '60s. I think it's of

great signficance that she was not involved in that culture: My sister

and I were not raised by a woman who was dropping acid at

Woodstock. We were raised by a woman who was wearing poodle

skirts in high school. It was a decade when President Harry Truman

delivered the first transcontinental television broadcast, Dwight

Eisenhower moved into the White House, the Korean War was fought,

Rosa Parks refused to give up her seat at the back of the bus, Dr. Jonas

Salk developed a polio vaccine, and National Airlines began the first

domestic jet airliner passenger service between New York City and

Miami. The '50s was the era of Lucille Ball, Dick Van Dyke, Ritchie

Valens, The Big Bopper, Howdy Doody, and The Lone Ranger.

Technically, Mom wasn't a Baby Boomer and wasn't raised in the '60s,

like most of my friends' parents. Contrast the culture of the '50s

conservative, adult-dominated World War II generation with that of

the '60s as the seventy million children from the post-war baby boom

became teenagers and young adults. The '60s was about Vietnam,

Camelot, Martin Luther King Jr., Andy Warhol, drugs, Elvis, the Beatles,

Jimi Hendrix, the Grateful Dead, police dogs, prayer in public schools

found unconstitutional, Muhammad Ali, and hippies. Those differences

aren't small progressions of similar beliefs. They mark a revolution of

ideas.

My sister was born in 1976 and I in 1973. Mom was raising us

from the experience and empirical knowledge of the '50s in Kansas.

She was a wonderful mother whose unconditional love was only equal

to her Pollyanna view of the world in which Jesus has a plan for us all,

is always in control, performs magical miracles, and sends believers to

heaven and everyone else to hell. We were Presbyterians but I couldn't

have told you why we weren't Methodists or another denomination.

Our religious view of the world came from Mom. I think mothers love

religion, especially Christianity, because they can't bear the concept of

their children dying and not having an afterlife. Why, of course, God

loves everyone unconditionally. We are all God's children and all

mothers love their children unconditionally. Certainly if we take

Thomas Anselm's definition of God as something "than which nothing

greater can be thought," unconditional love must be in the nature of

God . But, in our house, you had to believe in Jesus. Otherwise, you

were going to Hell to suffer for a bazillion million years, and that was

your fault, not God's fault. God gave you a book to follow. Instead, you

didn't choose the right God or the right part of his book. (Sorry, Jewish

friends, Mom meant the New Testament). So much for unconditional

love. I don't think my mother gave this part much thought. She likes

the self-righteousness of being one of the chosen. We used to pray

every night that all our Jewish friends would become Christian so they

didn't have to suffer eternal damnation.

Mom also taught us to sew. She taught us manners and sent me to finishing school. I shit you not. When I'm not starting fights now because of my difficulty reorienting to society, I have impeccable manners and can eat in perfect Continental or American style. Mom didn't want us watching movies or TV that would warp our brains or make us violent. She wouldn't hear of teenage drinking or drugs as opposed to most parents of the time who were products of the '60s and rather sure their teenagers were going to have a beer at a party.

But Mom also was an adventurer and cowgirl at heart. She grew up watching *The Lone Ranger*. She is a poet, photographer, and creative soul. She's whimsical and a free spirit, too. We did lots of crafts and were allowed to imagine and play. Compared to my father, she was a risk taker. When Mom decided where we were going on vacation, we would go west to Colorado for horseback riding and camping. When Dad decided, we'd head south to the Bahamas, Florida, or Cancun. After my parents divorced, Mom went on a stagecoach trip across Kansas and dog sledding in Colorado. Dad went on a cruise to Greece and bought a bigger boat in Fort Lauderdale.

So when I say that Dad bought Mom a farm in Lone Jack, Missouri, you can see he must have loved her. The farm included a fifteen-acre lake and a stream that wound through the rest of its sixty-one acres. We bought a rowboat so we could get around the lake and stream. We also had one of those 1980s conversion vans that we'd fill to the brim with camping equipment and park near the stream. We'd put up the tent, build a fire, and spend the weekend in nature. For my sister, that meant playing Tonto to my Lone Ranger. My job, as I saw it, was to hunt down and kill every snake I could find. Her job was to assist me. She didn't usually do her job. Why did I need to hunt and kill snakes? Seemed like a good job at the time, especially since snakes were known to be evil ever since they started all that bullshit with Eve and the apple.

That brings me to my utility belt. I deemed it necessary to carry a machete to hack away any bush into which a snake might decide to crawl. But I also needed a survival knife. Not a problem. Dad and I got matching ones for Christmas. Ever since *Rambo* and *First Blood*, all men know the importance of carrying a quality survival knife, complete with a compass. I also carried a gun — a pellet pistol when I was young and a .22 when I was older. Guns weren't a big deal to my sister or me because our dad had introduced us to them intelligently when we were young. Consequently, we didn't fear them because they were unknown to us. Nor did we have an unhealthy interest in them. When I was eight, Dad helped me hold his Colt Commander .45 pistol, which is really loud and makes a tremendous kick, or recoil, when fired. When he helped me hold and shoot it, the ferocity of the noise and kick from the exiting round scared the living crap out of me.

"Do you understand why you never play with guns now?" Dad asked.

"Yes, sir, I do," I replied.

Through the years, we shot all sorts of guns at the farm, and I became an expert in gun safety and a proficient shooter with both revolvers and semiautomatic pistols. I much preferred the .22, however, because it barely recoiled and was much easier for a boy to shoot. I wasn't allowed to walk around with a loaded gun, much to my dismay, but when I turned ten, I had my own pellet pistol, which uses air pressure to shoot a pointed pellet that can kill small birds or snakes. I never ever shot a bird, I would have cried to end its song. But I did shoot the hell out of snakes! I also had a pellet rifle, which was more accurate and better for shooting snakes from farther away.

Dad hated the farm. The whole thing made him nervous. But he packed us up and took us there a lot of weekends when I know he'd rather have been sitting in our gazebo back home with a glass of wine and a cigar, pondering Aristotle or Clint Eastwood's Dirty Harry — his two favorite philosophers.

Mom let me see myself as a hero, especially at the farm. Walking there, protecting us all from snakes, I was a knight fighting dragons, I was Saint George. I wanted to be seen as a hero, so the idea of doing things other people feared led me to believe I was showing great courage, and thusly, was one. David faced Goliath, Daniel slept in the lions' den, Joshua brought down Jericho: those were the stories of my childhood. Of course, to my Mom, who always saw me as a hero, I was the greatest of heroes: If I climbed a tree, she confirmed it was the tallest tree in the neighborhood. If I jumped my bike, she just knew I was the best bike rider on the street. When I jumped the Sea Doo, she would tell you I was head high to the boat's captain and she had the pictures to prove it. If I put on a cowboy hat, I looked tougher than John Wayne, and when I walked, I swaggered like Clint Eastwood. I could be president or I could be a superhero, but no matter what I did, Mom told me I did it the best. It gets difficult to keep topping your own accomplishments after a while. Also, when you're a kid, especially at five or six years old, your view of the world is clouded with the actual and the imaginary. You can be a hero or a cowboy, and your parents can do all sorts of things that seem quite powerful to you, like throwing a ball really far, driving a car, or changing a lightbulb. They also seem to know amazing and impossible things about how the world works, why dogs look funny when they poop, who God is, what exactly constitutes good and naughty behavior on Santa's List, where you can ride horses, and how to make boo-boos stop hurting with a kiss.

If I learned to be a hero at the farm, I believe I learned about justice from the great cartoon, *The Super Friends*, who lived or worked in the Hall of Justice. If your headquarters is the Hall of Justice, you presuppose everything you do will be in the pursuit of justice, and that you, by extension, are a just person. Justice, à la *Super Friends*, is very black and white: Good guys are famously good. Bad guys are famously bad. As Rudyard Kipling said, "East is East and West is West, and never the twain shall meet."

But as we grow older, justice tends to morph into the concept of Fairness. To be fair, you give your sister half. You got two cupcakes?

So will he. You punched me in the arm. I get to punch you in the arm but just once, or it's not fair. For teenagers, justice remains an ethereal concept that more closely resembles quality along with quantity: "Everyone else gets to go to the mall by themselves! Mom, you are so unfair!"

Of course, the Bible was an influence. We were not allowed to behave in certain ways or have certain feelings. 1 John 2:11 explained how bad things such as hate, revenge, and killing were of the devil. The passage says: "But he that hateth his brother, is in darkness, and walketh in darkness, and knoweth not whither he goeth; because the darkness hath blinded his eyes.(Douay-Rheims 1899 American Edition)." I grew up learning that hate was not an acceptable emotion to have in your heart. Jesus taught forgiveness and we were told to do what Jesus did—forgive our enemies. Come on, though. Who or what did I really hate growing up? Broccoli? The New York Yankees? My sister, because she ripped my comic book? Missing an episode of Scooby-Doo? Even we adults banter around the word "hate" to describe our strong dislike toward everything from taxes to rap music to Lindsay Lohan's new movie to war. Republicans hate Democrats. Democrats hate Republicans. We all hate politicians. We don't experience actual hate very often at all. Merriam Webster defines hate

as "intense hostility and aversion, usually deriving from fear, anger, or

sense of injury." But if you click on hate, defined for kids, you are back

to "a strong dislike."

The Bible is not clear on hate. The New Testament God pretty

much thinks hate is bad, as stated in 1 John 4:20 (Douay-Rheims 1899

American Edition):

If any man say, I love God, and hateth his brother; he is a liar. For

he that loveth not his brother, whom he seeth, how can he love God,

whom he seeth not?

Matthew 6:15 (Douay-Rheims 1899 American Edition) tells us:

But if you will not forgive men, neither will your Father forgive

you your offences.

The Old Testament God, on the other hand, hated some folks

very much. He made the poor Jews wander around for forty years in

the shitty-ass desert and he killed everything on the whole earth

except Noah and whatever he put on his boat. Proverbs 20:22 (Douay-

Rheims 1899 American Edition) is unequivocal:

Say not: I will return evil: wait for the Lord and he will deliver thee.

It's as if he's saying, "No, No. Don't you go hating on that man who was evil. Don't you go try to repay the evil. You just wait for your Father the Almighty to open up a can of all-powerful whupass on him. I drowned the whole world! Don't worry about it: I will fuck him up!" You don't want *that* God coming for you.

In all seriousness, all the above verses, and almost all others I was given to memorize, didn't really explain the emotion of hate or what one should do to avoid it. Instead, the Bible tells you what to do and the consequences of either doing or not doing it. With respect to hate, almost all the verses, such as the ones above, essentially say: don't hate or you are a douche bag and God will make your head fall off. Many researchers disagree on exactly which emotions are defined as the basic ones from which all other emotions emanate, though most concur that anger and fear fit the bill. We are all familiar with the flight or fight response activated by the hypothalamus that prepares our bodies to fight or flee in the face of danger. This physiological response seems to be a biological obstacle when it comes to avoiding emotions such as anger and fear. That is to say, when we perceive something that frightens us, we physiologically respond in a way

nature has found to be the most probable way to survive — flight or

flee (or, in the case of some animals that use camouflage, freeze).

When humans are presented with a potentially dangerous

situation, adrenaline floods the body in preparation for flight or fight.

A fight response can manifest in aggressive or angry behavior,

whereas flight may lead to an attempt to defuse the situation or seek

help. If prolonged, the fight or flight response suppresses the immune

system, leaving an individual vulnerable to a host of stress-related

diseases. Does this pre-programmed flight or fight behavior, which

may be aggressive and angry, lead to hate? If yes, could hate be a

natural reaction?

These are all adult questions, though. I was raised in Mom's

world, where God will always protect you, and I was raised in Dad's

world, a place where risk is measured and education is crucial. It's all

very clear and easy to follow when you are ten years old. In Kansas.

With no gray areas. And you're Christian. And you have money. Back

then, I didn't know about the abyss that Nietzsche spoke of, and I

hadn't ever seen any monsters.

Chapter 2:

The Police Academy

"In youth we learn; in age we understand."

— Marie von Ebner-Eschenbach

November 1996, Nashville

I had no idea what to expect on the first day of the Police

Academy. Nashville, Tennessee had a Metropolitan Police Department,

meaning the whole county was treated as a city, so the department

(we were called "Metro") was fairly large at fourteen hundred sworn officers. According to all the reports at the time, though, it was understaffed by about three hundred. The Police Academy campus begins with a long road that winds uphill from a large gate to a building, looking very much like an elementary school, at the top. That hill, incidentally, would become familiar as punishment for various officer trainee infractions.

To the left of the main building was a large shooting range. Behind it was a large paved oval driving track, about a half mile in diameter, used for various high-speed and defensive driving classes. On one side of the track was a hangar for helicopters with various unimaginative designations such as Air 1, Air 2, and Air 3. We officers just called them all "Air 1," which was funny for some reason, On the other side of the driving track was an area allotted for the K-9 Building and Training Course. The whole complex made me proud to be a part of the Metro PD.

We were required to be in our formation in the gym at 0700 hours. That's when inspection would take place. We were taught all the military marching and parade maneuvers, including standing at attention for inspection. The Marine and Army guys in my class said the Academy was pretty much like boot camp, but with a police theme.

Clearly, they had a step up on someone coming from an academic

environment, and it took me months to get comfortable with the

standards necessary to please the instructors. Two glaring words in

my file become like a huge target on my back: Vanderbilt University.

You might as well have dropped me off in the Serengeti dressed like an

antelope and poured maple syrup all over me. I was immediately

referred to as "Vanderbilt," had to refer to myself as Officer Trainee

Vanderbilt, and was targeted for failure. While Vanderbilt was ranked

the seventeenth best university in the United States at the time, it was

even more well known in its Nashville home as an academic

powerhouse. So I was deemed a nerd who neither should, nor could,

survive to become a full police officer.

But I also was a Division I soccer scholarship athlete who

played my sophomore year with a broken wrist, broken ankle, and

twenty-nine stitches in my face. I'd had two wake-up-in-the-hospital

concussions and I played goalkeeper, which meant I was half crazy,

anyway. I was no pansy-ass nerd who was going to let anyone break

me of anything. So a battle ensued: I was trying to keep from making

constant mistakes in an unfamiliar military environment. The

instructors were trying to break me down and force me to quit. There was one, in particular, whom I loved but who was determined to make

my life hell. How? Various annoying ways. I always had "invisible" lint,

as we called it, on my uniform. My boots were never perfect. My eyes

weren't staring perfectly ahead. My hat was crooked. I would breathe

too loud, stand too imperfectly, do something, not do something, stand

up too slow, stand up too fast, not yell my name loud enough, not look

confident enough, look too confident, played soccer, went to

Vanderbilt, forget that "Vanderbilt sucks at football," not say

"Vanderbilt sucks" loud enough, not "truly believe in my heart

Vanderbilt sucks," not "truly believe I suck at life," and on and on. The

point was to make the world we were living in unpredictable and

inconsistent. They did a very good job.

Now, I found all of this an amusing game I tried to win by

making it harder for them to "gig" me on some detail. I figured if they

had to make up something ridiculous to force me to run to the

academy entrance carrying my desk, do push-ups, run around the

helicopter pad, or run around the building while chanting "Vanderbilt

sucks ass," then I had won that day. This is not to say I was the only

one who was picked on. Far from it. Class after class, however, the

statistics bore out the instructors: 35-40 percent of the class would fail. So it was of paramount importance for them to weed out the

weaker candidates. Anyone they felt couldn't psychologically or

physically handle the stress of police work was intimidated, pushed,

cajoled, embarrassed, or forced to quit. Instructors also could

"persuade" trainees to leave.

The class work was easy for me, but I will say the law was the

most difficult part of the course academically. We had to know

criminal law better than lawyers or judges, in my humble opinion,

because we had to make split-second decisions in applying the law to

situations, people, circumstances, and our own behavior. We didn't

have the opportunity to research or send an intern to figure out if we

could arrest or shoot someone. A lot of people failed the law portion.

Predominantly, though, people just quit because the environment was

extremely tense and, if the instructors sensed you were weak, they

went for your jugular. A Vanderbilt graduate seemed like a weak,

academic nerd who lived in la-la land and could be broken. Now, I did

live in la-la land. I was, in fact, the head la-la at the time. I truly thought

this was a wonderful game and couldn't wait to get the toys and the

Batman Belt. But six months is a long time to be indoctrinated in a

highly stressful environment with a group of eighty alpha males.

(There were five females in the class, but they weren't involved in the constant battle to determine the alpha male, with all the fighting and peeing on trees.) I knew I didn't have the military background needed to take my turn being in charge of the class as Class Leader or even Squad leader. (There are four squads in a class.) But a lot of the alphas did have the background and wanted to prove their leadership abilities.

Our class leader was a Marine who was the best shot in the class and had a quiet but stern way about him. He made sure the squad leaders saw to it that the rest of us were perfectly groomed with our hats set perfectly on our heads and our boots perfectly shined. When we failed, he failed. We liked him, so we worked hard not to disappoint him or force the wrath of the instructors onto his head for our mistakes.

I combated constant humiliation attempts, badgering, and physical and mental stress by deciding to wear a cowboy hat, which, I want you to understand, was a great call. I didn't wear it during the twelve hours at the Academy, mind you. At night I would come home to my little condo where my puppy Black Lab, Gunner, was waiting (neither patiently, nor quietly, having created some sort of disaster after the dog walker left and before I returned). I would put on jeans

and my black Stetson, take Gunner to the nearby river to swim and

play, and then return home, where we would eat some pizza and dog

food. Chuck Norris wore a cowboy hat in a lot of his movies, and, of

course, Clint Eastwood was "the man with no name" in all the great

Spaghetti Westerns. I was no different: a man with his dog, preparing

to be a cop fighting for justice. So why wouldn't I be wearing a similar

black Stetson? What was one to wear, if not a proper outfit becoming a

hero? Behold our hero. As Mr. Fabian says in *Tombstone*, he is "the

quintessential frontier type. Note the lean silhouette... eyes closed by

the sun, though sharp as a hawk. He's got the look of both predator and

prey."

On Friday nights I'd put on my boots and hat and saunter

(sometimes drive) to the local watering hole known as the Bellevue

Pub. I drank Budweiser in a bottle and listened to the music and

sometimes karaoke. I didn't know anyone from Nashville: after I

graduated, my girlfriend dumped me, my friends left, and my parents

were in the midst of their World War III divorce back in Kansas City.

So I went to the bar to be around people who weren't yelling at me for

various infractions. But the point is, as it should always be, the outfit. I was playing the part I wanted to play, another great role from childhood fantasy — half cop, half cowboy. I was Ryan starring in his make-believe show as Chuck Norris Eastwood Schwarzenegger. The one downside to the Academy was the money. Earning a total of $714 every two weeks is poverty. It also was my introduction to managing money, stretching money, and just trying to live on that kind of income. I had grown up in a 4,500-square-foot house with a three-car garage. I did not come from humble beginnings, as everyone likes to claim. I had absolutely no idea how to manage money that wasn't enough money for whatever you needed. I learned what happened when you ran out of money. Bringing home $1,400 a month and paying $600 in rent wasn't easy. In three months, my electricity was turned off. Three weeks later, having borrowed $100 from an Academy classmate, I got Nashville Electric to turn it back on. That was a good but tough lesson in personal finance. The home front was good, though. I had a new girlfriend named Susan and Gunner and I had each other, and all three of us played a lot at the river.

Ultimately, the Police Academy had four very interesting phases mixed with a great deal of academic work and fitness.

The first interesting part was shooting a gun. I had learned to shoot growing up at our sixty-one-acre property, so I was a good

enough shot to begin with. We spent only three weeks at the range,

learning to become proficient with a Glock .40-caliber pistol and

Remington 870 shotgun. We participated in stress courses during

which we'd move toward a series of targets while being sprayed with

water even as sirens sounded, smoke grenades went off, and an

instructor screamed in our ears. We practiced drawing from the

holster and firing, since the holsters had various security snaps

engaged when the gun was properly secured. At the end of the three

weeks, I was near the top of the class but by no means the best.

Perhaps I was tenth out of seventy officer trainees. My new best friend,

Randy, and a couple of ex-Marines were the best shooters. After the

weeks at the range, we were allowed to carry our empty Glocks in our

holsters on our gun belt. I won't lie. We felt a little bit more important.

The second interesting part of the Academy was learning to

drive like crazy people. We learned to do reverse hundred and eighty

degree turns: that's when the vehicle is in reverse and you throw the

wheel around, slam the car into drive, and nail the accelerator again,

so that you're going forward in the direction in which you were just

driving in reverse. Just like the movies! We also chased each other around the track in shitty Ford LTDs, learning how to initiate a pursuit,

follow vehicles appropriately, and keep the driver side window away

from gunfire if a runner shoots back at you.

When we learned to execute tactical traffic stops, we watched

disturbing video footage of cops being killed on traffic stops. One video

still stops my blood because the officer was wearing a microphone.

You watch as the guy shoots the cop, who couldn't be more than

twenty years old. Then the guy comes over as the cop, lying on the

ground, pleads with him to let him live, begs him. The guy shoots the

cop in the head. Then you listen to his breathing stop and watch him

die. At the Academy, that video was the first thing that shook me up. It

was quite a little espresso shot of reality into my giant role-playing

adventure.

The third interesting part was fighting, the only thing with

which I wasn't familiar in any real way. I had my share of the scrapes

any boy or guy experiences while going through high school and

college. I wasn't a wilting flower, so there had been a couple. At the

Academy, we trained in boxing and some martial arts, but those were

boring. The two lessons that stood out were both taught by Sgt. Mason

Green, who later would become my narcotics sergeant and idol. He was a big, scary man. There weren't just stories about him. There were

legends. One day, I had to fight him while he was wearing a big, red

padded suit. We were learning to use our ASP batons — the kind

everyone carries now. They snap out and extend eighteen inches. We

were supposed to hit him in non-lethal areas — knees, elbows, and

wrists. After we hit him enough times, we were to give him the

command, "Put your hands behind your back!" Then, the plan was, he

would lie down and we would handcuff him.

What we didn't know at the time was that this engagement was

called a "failure drill" in which everything we did was going to fail. It

was a chance to experience what it's like to start getting your ass

kicked while panic set in and your heart rate shot through the roof. We

had to overcome that panic and think of a solution. We had to keep

fighting, no matter what.

The training officers were trying to put our minds into what

they called "Condition Black." They were also trying to affect our

"normalcy bias" by creating a situation in which we were forced to

escalate the level of violence to its maximum lethal response. Our job

was to manage the mental shock of this violent confrontation and stop

ourselves from entering "Condition Black." Most everyone experiences

"Condition Black," a mental state in which the brain rejects the

scenario at hand and refuses to think. Normalcy bias is what gets

people killed during natural disasters, airplane crashes, and other

emergency situations. People reject the danger at hand and soothe

themselves with the idea that the situation just can't be that bad. More

than 70 percent of survivors in the Twin Towers on 9/11 reported

talking with other people about what they all should do before

evacuating, according to TIME magazine. When people have not

experienced a trauma, or in the case of unprecedented disaster, they

tend to underestimate and diminish the danger of the situation. Take

that concept and pair it with the psychological conditions of readiness

that law enforcement uses to describe kinds of situational tactical

awareness, as taught by the late Jeff Cooper:

White = Total disregard for one's surroundings. Think sheep

eating grass.

Yellow = Steady, cautious awareness of an environment. A

person is on the lookout for danger.

Orange = Hyper vigilance in an environment. When a bad thing

is detected, a person gets ready to act.

Red = Go time. A person is completely focused and takes immediate, decisive action.

Black = Freeze time. A person is assaulted. The color refers to the blackness of death.

Condition white transitions to condition black. Condition yellow transitions to condition orange, which becomes condition red at the right time, before going back down to orange, and then yellow. Research suggests that even when the brain is calm, it takes eight to ten seconds to process new information. Stress slows the process. When the brain cannot find an acceptable response to a situation, it fixates on a single and sometimes default solution that may or may not be correct. In everyday life, most people are in condition white. Therefore, they quickly jump to condition black because of the brain's inability to react to extreme stress quickly. When they do manage to recognize a dangerous situation, normalcy bias causes cognitive dissonance and individuals underestimate the situation, often not reacting or reacting inappropriately.

So in this drill, Sgt. Green wasn't going to give up and another sergeant, Sgt. Tom, was going to attack as well, when he felt he had sufficient surprise. I gave commands to Sgt. Green, but he failed to

respond to any of them. I threw a couple of punches at him as he

squared up to attack. I snapped out my baton and began re-issuing

commands with the threat of my strike clear. Of course, per the drill,

he continued his attack forward and really tried to hit me, which I

expected. Suddenly, Sgt Green, who owned a karate school, knocked

the air out of me with a front kick right into my sternum. Then he

really began attacking me, punching me again in the kidney. I

disengaged, spun around, and tried to strike him low in the side of the

knee. The baton had no effect on the giant in the foam suit and he just

kept coming at me, again and again. At this point my heart was racing

and I was unsure what to do to stop him. I just kept trying to get my

breath back and struck him every time he came in for an attack. I was

ineffective defending myself against him.

He had almost disabled my left leg with several kicks to the

nerve cluster in the side of my thigh and I continued to strike him

every time he got close. Just when I was disoriented and clearly

beginning to struggle, Sgt. Tom, who had been screaming at me,

jumped in and attempted to tackle me! At this point, as much as I knew

this was all occurring in the gym of the police academy, the drill was having the desired effect. I was beginning to panic and wasn't sure

how to handle the situation. I assumed, incorrectly, that this was going

to be a basic boring liability drill where we had to comply with federal

or state guidelines for some liability reason. This situation was turning

into something way different! I was in front of my class getting my ass

kicked, which, in addition to the embarrassment factor, wasn't feeling

feel very good physically or in terms of my self-confidence. I dodged

Sgt Tom's tackle and struck him with the baton in the back as he went

under and by me. I was in a panic and finally my brain clicked in: There

were two assailants, two people capable of bringing me down

individually, let alone when combined. This was a deadly force drill. I

stepped back as quickly as possible, dropped my baton, drew my

simunitions gun (think paintball but more realistic), and yelled, "Get

on the ground or I shoot!" Both sergeants dropped to their knees and

the drill ended after they complied with all my handcuffing

instructions. I'd made it through.

Over the next several days, I enjoyed watching the rest of the

class go through the drill as I had, with no knowledge of the conditions

or the circumstances, and having to find their own way to success.

Some failed the drill and ultimately washed out of the class. The intensity of those types of drills created stress that trainees simply did not want to deal with in training, and certainly, in reality. As for me, that drill would save my life about seven months from that day.

The fourth phase I found intriguing was role playing. Actors played various roles in different scenarios staged at offices and places around the Academy grounds and we trainees would respond as if the events were real. The actors had a lot of fun watching us try to solve the problems in much the same way it's fun to watch the scene in *Bambi* when the little guy skids and slides as he tries to walk on ice.

Several of the actors were cops who came back to haze or help wreck us as well as for the free booze and awesome DUI opportunity. We got to do real sobriety tests because some of the actors and off-duty cops had gotten various levels of drunk while we were in classes that day. We'd pull them over on the track and have to run them through the gamut of drunk tests, then guesstimate their sobriety level as close as we could between .03 and 1.5. A final breath analyzer would confirm how well or poorly we guessed. Mostly, those guys just loved getting drunk and, in the domestic violence portion, acting as much like an asshole as the typical guy in a real domestic. I was dying to come back and do the same when I was eligible!

The role playing was always tedious in that, time and time again, we were forced to handcuff, give commands, and keep control of various situations. If you looked past the monotony of the textbook-like scenarios, however, it became apparent, at least to me, that while the law was very straightforward, applying it was a whole different game. It was easy for me to extrapolate every situation into one where the threads were tangled into a substantial mess with no good solution. I could see, for instance, how every domestic had the potential of becoming a no-win situation if no one wanted to leave the premises and neither party was guilty of anything. According to the law, someone has to leave. Common sense even tells you that you'll be back if someone doesn't leave. What to do? I'll tell you a secret: most guys, including me, handle such a scenario by saying, "If I come back here tonight, both of you are going to jail." That method works a lot, especially when both parties are high or drunk and don't want to go jail. All in all, the role playing in the Academy helped me learn how very quickly normal situations can become chaotic and dangerous. Each situation was engineered to be a textbook case. I could imagine how quickly conditions could spiral out of control when the situations involved real people with violent solutions, drugs and alcohol were involved, or emotions were escalated.

As for traffic stops, we'd play the bad guys on the traffic stop for each other and almost always succeeded in killing the cop trainees. We'd sit in the car on the track and they would pull us over and walk up to the car. Since everyone wanted to shoot each other as much as possible with the simunitions guns (again, think paintball), every traffic stop would turn into a gunfight. When I was playing the bad guy, I liked to comply with the cop trainee all the way up until the part when I gave him my driver's license. Then I'd shoot him through the rolled down window. This one trainee, Jeff, would pull over and wait for you to get out of your car. When you got halfway to the trunk, he would lean out the window and shoot you. It was brutal. One of my favorite moves was being the passenger and waiting for the trainee to just about get to the driver side window. Then I'd jump out, run around the back of the car, and shoot him. We were very creative and the point was easy to make: Traffic stops were immensely dangerous. You had damned well be ready for anything or you weren't going to make very many before you made your last. That lesson would save my life a couple of times.

For example, about a year or so after my bank robber shooting, I made another one-of-a-hundred-that -month "routine" traffic stops.

Have you ever walked into a familiar place before and known – *just known* – that something was out of place, that something was just … wrong? Maybe you came home from work to your apartment and the pattern on your couch pillow was turned the wrong direction. Or maybe you walked into your office and the picture of your family was tilted the wrong way. Or maybe you came home one day and nothing was out of place, but the hair on the back of your neck stood up. Have you ever awakened in the middle of the night and listened quietly for a repeat of the sound that you know *must* have startled you from sleep?

I hit the blue lights of my police car on Trinity Lane at about 2:30 in the morning. The sky was moonless that night and Trinity Lane was deserted. I left the Vice Office to rendezvous with a friend working E detail (7:30 p.m.-4:00 a.m.) back toward downtown Nashville. I was only about ten minutes away from downtown when I hit the lights. I don't remember why I stopped the car. I don't even remember what kind of car it was. But I remember it was navy blue, and I remember pointing my spotlight through the back windshield and into the rearview mirror to blind the driver as I approached, just as I'd been taught in the Academy, just as I'd done a hundred times before. I radioed myself out to the dispatcher and kept my eyes on the interior of the car I had pulled over, looking for any furtive, suspicious movement. I remember clearly, very clearly, that I saw no suspicious movement.

As I stepped out of my vehicle, though, that "feeling" came upon me. The hair on the back of my neck stood up as I exited my car and stepped into the dark night. I stopped after I exited and stepped back so I was behind my open police car door. I stood, wondering what was triggering my fear sensation and staring into the dark, looking for that tiny bit of ominous motion I must have seen and listening for that little sound I must registered on some level. I decided to walk around my car – out of the driver's sight – and approach his car from the passenger side. Drivers seem to do one of two things when they get pulled over: some root around for their wallet and insurance card while glancing in the side or rearview mirror to see the officer approach, while others stare straight ahead and make no unnecessary movement because they don't want to surprise the officer or make him/her nervous by reaching a hand into the glove compartment or a pocket. This guy was not moving. He was just staring outside his driver side window. Knowing that was wrong, I drew my gun and

continued creeping up the passenger side with my flashlight

off until I was near his rear-passenger door window and could

see inside. His back was turned toward me because he was

pointing a gun out his window.

I guess I could have shot him. Now, years later, I

probably would have. But I was young and still raw from my

bank robber shooting. I chose to walk slowly back behind my

vehicle and call in on the radio. A number of police cars pulled

up in front and back and the suspect was taken into custody

without incident. To this day I remember those silly academy

traffic stop games where we all tried to kill each other for fun

to make each other remember to always expect anything. I

don't know what I saw that night, but I'm glad I saw it. Maybe

you can remember this story the next time you get pulled over

and think the cop should somehow know you are a good

person.

The whole Academy experience was a wonderful game for me

and, at the end of the six months, I was certain I was ready for the

street, just like every other naive officer trainee. I was truly going to

fight evil. I was a Jedi Knight! I was Batman! I was all the heroes of my youth. I can't tell you how excited and proud I was to have graduated.

My mom and sister flew to Nashville for the ceremony, and my mom

pinned the badge on me as I received it, standing proudly in my dress

blues. I was Badge 93114. We went to dinner afterward, too. I wore my

loaded gun for the first time with my badge clipped on my belt. I wore

cowboy boots and an untucked long sleeve shirt, too—a red shirt,

exactly like Mel Gibson wore in *Lethal Weapon*. My Shakespearean

flaw had reared its ugly head: I thought this was a game, and games

were for winning. Heroes won. So I did more than survive. I was in the

top of my class, winning an award for placing second in academics and

another for placing first in physical fitness. *Hmm,* I wondered, *what

else could I do to get an award while on the street?* Thank God I'd be

working for six months with field training officers. The day I realized

awards were given out as ribbons to wear on your uniform probably

was the most dangerous —day of my life.

   I looked down at my silver badge and out at some of the older

officers, all sergeants and lieutenants. The space above my badge was

blank, blue material. Above their badges were ribbons of different

colors representing different accomplishments and honors. I wanted

the recognition they got by virtue of a glance at their uniforms. I thought they must have been beaming with pride to have those

ribbons. Of course, the opportunity cost for a ribbon is a memory,

sometimes a crippling one. The opportunity costs of actions that would

get you a ribbon from the mayor were high. Ribbons were given for

heroic deeds, which oftentimes meant surviving. But I didn't know that

then. I was in pursuit of ribbons. So, yeah, I would work hard for them

so everyone could see them on my uniform and know what kind of cop

I was. Everyone would know I was a hero. What I couldn't see was that

I would trade my soul for ribbons. Dad would not approve. How many

ribbons is a soul worth?

Chapter 3:

My Vest: Part I

You can get help from teachers, but you are going to have to learn a lot by yourself, sitting alone in a room.

—Dr. Seuss

April 1997, Nashville, Tennessee

My bulletproof vest was itchy. Under it I wore a white tee shirt , as everyone did, but it still was smashing down my chest hair. It also was always too tight or too loose. A vest has two straps that come across the midriff (one around the chest and the other just above the

belly button) and two that go over the shoulders. The two on the

shoulders always choked me and wouldn't sit properly above my gun

belt. I also couldn't get the two around my chest not to cut off my

breath, or conversely, be too loose. *Stupid, heavy thing. Ugh.*

Anyway, roll call is very much like all the cliché roll calls on TV,

but more boring. My very first one was at 1430 hours on a Tuesday. I

found out my field training officer was Jim Kennedy, a twenty-year

veteran. He looked at me like every senior has ever looked at any

freshman, and it wasn't confidence building. Jim was handsome with a

great head of silver hair any man would like to have when he's about

forty-five. He had patrolled the South Sector of Nashville for almost all

of his twenty years, and knew just about everything there was to know

about the five to ten square miles of his 11 Zone. I wanted to drive. Jim

made it clear I would never drive. He also didn't want me to touch the

radio or play with the siren. How cliché is that? Also, his utility belt

didn't resemble mine at all. The Metropolitan Nashville Police

Department wore very dark blue uniforms and silver badges. We

didn't have to wear ties or hats, so we wore white tee shirts

underneath our bulletproof vests. Our utility belts, also known as gun belts, were made of a shiny material style that looked like black patent

leather. Jim's gun belt held his holster, ASP baton, dual magazine case,

handcuff case, and radio holster – the minimum items required, per

policy. This was back in the day when our radios could actually be

used as weapons because of their size . Many a radio has been thrown

at many a fleeing person, or so I've heard. Sometimes Jim stuck a

flashlight in his back pocket.

While looking at Jim's belt, my first thought was that he in no

way was as prepared as I was. If he had engaged as many aliens,

villains, and Russians as I had in my backyard, he would have added

more stuff. I was mightily aware of Batman's amazing ability to pull

the right thing from his belt during any given confrontation, and I was

most definitely of the Batman School of Thought. My belt had a Level

III holster, dual magazine pouch, extra single magazine pouch, two

handcuff cases, a flashlight holder, a flashlight ring to hold my larger

mag light, radio holster, ASP baton, car key holder (which was

irrelevant because Jim wouldn't let me drive, anyway), and

Leatherman utility tool. I also carried a backup Glock 27 on my left

ankle and knives clipped to both pants pockets.

Inside my shirt, attached to my bulletproof vest, was another knife and another 12-round magazine.

Lastly, my Academy class— Session 32: "With Discipline and Pride our Blood runs Blue, Together as One, We're Session 32"—was the first to be issued OC/CS pepper spray, which burns your eyes horribly and tears them up so you have difficulty seeing. We had to be sprayed a couple of times during the academy (and every subsequent year) and I can tell you it sucks big time. Though the effects differ for everyone, my eyes teared, burned, and shut, my face burned like hell, and my snout ran like a waterfall. So I had the spray on my belt, at the front belt buckle, too. As you can clearly see, I was totally prepared for any situation I would encounter. This was a wonderful game, and I had a fantastic costume.

My first day was a rather normal patrol day. I don't remember any of the day before lunch at Waffle House on Harding Road. Jim always had lunch at the Waffle House at 4 p.m. on Tuesdays. I was concentrating mostly on remembering the street names as we drove. At the Academy, they emphasized always remembering the name of the street you were on, in case you needed help. At the time, I thought that was pretty obvious, but driving around a brand new area, I realized I couldn't remember jack shit. Our first call was at a

Vietnamese house on a street where a couple of gangs had established

a presence, so it was dangerous. But not to me. I was a combination of

completely petrified and dumbstruck way past talking or looking like I

had any clue as to what I was doing. Jim was cautious; I was glad to

finally be wearing a real live utility belt like Batman.

I remember how weird it was the first time I walked into a

house where everyone was yelling at each other, at us, at whatever. I

decided I should stand behind Jim and remain silent. My only

experience with this type of situation was from the Academy where

actors helped you resolve real-life scenarios. That was not like this.

This situation included a bleeding woman, a very pissed-off father and

mother, and a brother or two, all screaming in Vietnamese and broken

English. Jim figured out they were screaming about the suspect, who

apparently was upstairs and didn't see why he couldn't knock around

his girlfriend or fiancée a little bit, just like in the old country. I

followed Jim upstairs. He said, "Get ready to get him."

Now, for those of you unfamiliar with domestic violence law, it

was changed in the '90s with the Violence Against Women Act to really

protect women too scared to prosecute their boyfriends and husbands

for fear of retribution and other obvious reasons. Nothing is more frustrating to cops than seeing a beaten woman and not being able to do much about it if she decided not to prosecute. Her boyfriend, who, she knew, would take a shovel to her head if she said anything, would smugly stand by and corroborate her story that she knocked out her teeth while falling down the stairs in their one-story home. Police officers can prosecute felonies on the basis of probable cause and don't need the corroboration of a witness or victim. In other words, if we cops have sufficient reason to believe that a crime has been committed and that you committed it, we can arrest you. Domestic assault, however, is not a felony: it's a misdemeanor. The new domestic violence law made domestic violence an exception to the normal misdemeanor statute requiring the victim, or a witness, to prosecute. What does that mean? If police believe you are the perpetrator of a domestic violence assault, you are going to jail. Period. The way that worked out in real life was this: If one guy had a mark, cut or bruise, the other guy went to jail. If they both had a mark, they both went.

This gal's eye looked like Rocky Balboa's after Clubber Lang bitch slapped him around the ring in *Rocky III*. So we went upstairs to do one thing—arrest the guy. Now, the interesting thing about arresting someone is this: Saying "You're under arrest" is one thing when the guy replies, "OK." It's quite another when he replies, "Fuck

you." In essence, you can only arrest someone if you can make him

submit to your will. That's just what I was philosophizing about when

Jim said, "Get ready to get him." The "get ready" part was quite clear,

but I felt I needed a point of clarification on the prepositional phrase

"to get."

Looking back, I can only assume Jim was much readier than I

was for the chair that came flying through the air, quickly followed by

a brass lamp, which, thankfully for me, was not real brass. The chair

interrupted my attempt to remember when to read someone his

Miranda rights. The lamp cleared up my confusion. I now understood

the concept of "getting him" better. I still didn't, however, have any

idea what to do to "get him." Jim moved left and took out his ASP

baton. I remember thinking, *Wow, is Jim really going to hit him?* The

thought itself was, I admit, a distraction from the goal of "getting him,"

which was what I was supposed to be doing. At that point, all my

Academy training—countless hours of martial arts, grappling

techniques, handcuffing techniques, and takedown methods—were

completely overridden by the old fallback training all boys get

whenever a football is around: Attack the running back! Kill the guy with the football! So I tackled the suspect. I think he was distracted

while he wondered, as I did, if Jim was going to hit him.

Chapter 4:

The Good Cop

"We do not remember days, we remember moments."

— Cesare Pavese

April 1997, Nashville

To this day, I think about Anthony Franklin and I wonder if he thinks about me.-Sometimes, the most interesting things happen at the beginning, and my second day on the job proved that corollary true.

After roll call, we drove (that means Jim drove) to the Waffle

House again, where, I was informed, we also have lunch at 4 p.m. Wednesdays. That day, we met Officer Mike Keller. It's important at this point to establish that I was about five foot eight and one hundred fifty pounds at the time while wearing a belt second only to that of Batman. I was no Incredible Hulk. Officer Keller was. He had the biggest arms I've ever seen, and a mustache even a porn star would envy. Keller was about six foot one, though he seemed about 6 foot 10, and weighed about two hundred thirty, but the man was thick. When he wore short sleeve shirts, his arms looked like tree trunks sticking out of Navy tubes. Keller's gun belt was old school. He carried a holster, one pair of handcuffs, and his dual magazine case. In one back pocket, he carried his radio, and in the other a slap jack—a leather batting weapon the size and shape of a large serving spoon with a leather-encased lead head and the rest serving as a handle. When you slap someone with it, the motion whips the lead spoon part into a nasty weapon capable of breaking bones. Suffice it to say, police have not been allowed to carry them probably since the days of John Dillinger or Wyatt Earp. Keller sat with us, almost taking up the whole booth, looked at Jim, and asked, "Is this your rookie?"

"Yep", Jim drawled in his Nashville accent., "A Vanderbilt grad, too." Jim smiled at this description of me. I sensed that, again, my

education was about to be used against me.

"A Philosophy major," I stated, proudly.

Keller regarded me, leaned over the table, and said, "My

philosophy is this: you should be able to rape a man your same size."

I took in good faith that Keller probably could – and just may

have – raped a man his same size, and I decided to shut the fuck up for

the rest of lunch. After eating, we began the route Jim liked to go,

checking on certain businesses in 11 Zone, then moving up into 21

Zone, which was almost all Hispanic, specifically Mexican. Jim

patrolled 21 Zone, too, because he always had patrolled that area

before the powers that be decided to carve it out of 11 Zone, give it a

new number, and assign another car to patrol it. Jim didn't give a shit

what boundaries they drew. In his mind, it was 11 Zone. While

patrolling 21 Zone, we saw a young black man walking through a

basketball court in a small park just off Nolensville Road. Come to find

out, a black guy in this neighborhood would never happen. We were in

an all-Hispanic gang area with some Asian gangs mixed in. MS-13,

Asian Pride, Brown Pride, and Sur 13 pretty much ran the drugs and guns in the area and none of these groups would allow a young black male to hang out on their turf on their basketball court. No way. Not ever. Jim decided we needed to find out what was going on and probably save the guy from getting assaulted or worse. Also, stopping would be a great chance to show his rookie how a Terry stop is done.

We parked by the basketball court and exited our vehicle. Jim asked the guy where he was from. Meanwhile, I was quite excited to use all my Sherlock Holmes training to attempt to deduce if a crime was afoot and/or what the hell to do. My position was tactically perfect, I must say. As Jim faced our young rum scullion, I took up a position in front of and to the right of Jim, forcing our suspect to turn his head to glance at each of us. It said in one of the books at the Academy that this was important. As a Vanderbilt grad, I remembered what was in books. I also was in a great position if a gunfight broke out, like at the O.K. Corral: the suspect couldn't get both of us before one of us could get him. Frankly, I was congratulating myself on what a quality tactical position I had assumed as Jim continued to question him.

"Where are you from?" he asked.

"Felicia Street," the man replied. Possible, but it was on the other side of Nashville, near the Preston Taylor projects. The guy was probably no angel.

"What are you doing around here?" Jim probed.

"Visiting my sister," he responded. Possible, if she was Hispanic or he got lost.

"Oh," said Jim. "How did you get here from Felicia Street"?

"I walked," our guy said. Possible but very unlikely because it was a three- to four-hour walk.

"Where does your sister live?" Jim asked.

"I don't know," our guy replied.

"Going to be tough to get there, don't you think?" Jim asked. He loved sarcasm.

"What's your name?" Jim continued. Simple question. Later, I would find out people are good at quickly making up stories but not at making up names.

"Tony Sanchez."

"Spell it."

"S-A-N-D-C-H-E-S-S."

"Interesting spelling", Jim said. "What's in your pocket?" Our subject was wearing baggy jeans, tennis shoes, and a quarter zip starter jacket of a pro sports team, which had a big pocket in the front. Inside the pocket was an object whose weight clearly pulled down the front of the jacket.

"What do ya' got in the front pocket of that jacket?" Jim repeated. At that point a look came over our guy's face that I later would come to recognize as a very dangerous moment for a cop. It's the look of someone who thinks he's outsmarting the police and will be home free if only he can stay cool for just a little bit more—and then realizes he's fucked.

I think Antonio Sanchez Franklin—that was his real name— was going to shoot Jim at that point. He just kept glancing at my hand, which was loosely but obviously draped on the handle of my holstered gun. I think, in retrospect, he sure wishes he would have tried.

Instead, he turned and ran. Two things were against him. One, he was trying to get his gun out of his front pocket while he ran. Two,

no way in hell was I, who had just won the physical fitness award at

the Academy and who was a scholarship athlete in soccer and who was

in his first foot chase, going to lose this race. I tackled him in the corner

of the basketball court. Now this was fun! Just like an action hero! I

didn't know what to do after I'd tackled Franklin; it was very much a

situation of the dog catching the car. I was too naïve to realize he was

still going for his gun to shoot me. I thought we were just wrestling as

he tried to resist me. Thank God Jim arrived a couple of seconds later

to help keep Franklin under control and get him in cuffs. Handcuffing

him hadn't occurred to me. At that point, my jaws were clamped down

on the bumper with no real plan.

Franklin had in his possession a revolver, some jewelry, and

other trinkets that made it seem like we'd caught a burglary suspect.

Come to find out, however, he had had a busy morning before

stumbling upon us. On that day, April 18, 1997, at about 2 a.m. in

Dayton, Ohio, firefighters found the bodies of Ivory and Ophelia

Franklin shortly after arriving at the couple's burning house. Two

hours later, they found the body of Anthony Franklin—son of Ivory

and Ophelia and uncle of Antonio. Good ol' Antonio had burned the house down, and Uncle Anthony's body was almost ashes from the heat of the fire. All three had been beaten with a baseball bat. Ophelia, his grandma, also had been shot in the face. Ivory and Anthony Franklin died of blunt force trauma and smoke inhalation, so they probably lay there unconscious and then died. An autopsy revealed that either the gunshot wound or blunt force injuries could have killed Ophelia. It was at that point Antonio Sanchez Franklin fled to Nashville, where we found him at about 6 p.m. CST. When we arrested him, he was carrying his grandfather's loaded .38 revolver, which he had used to shoot his grandmother.

A jury in Montgomery County, Ohio, found Franklin guilty on seven counts of aggravated arson, six counts of aggravated murder, and two counts of aggravated robbery. He was sentenced to die for the aggravated murder charges and received ninety-one years in prison for the other offenses. The Supreme Court of Ohio denied his appeal in 2002. As of this writing, Antonio Sanchez Franklin sits on death row in Ohio.

To me, the whole thing was as real as the aliens and Russians I used to shoot in my backyard, except now I got to chase them. I thought about what had transpired, about the weight of a death penalty conviction. But, to be honest, the arrest of a real, live, evil

person just made the whole job seem that much more of a fun game. I

mean, a triple homicide suspect? On my second day? That was Jim's

biggest arrest in twenty-five years. I thought every day was going to be

that fun. I was actively battling evil and winning. Already.

Chapter 5:

The Fool

True patriotism hates injustice in its own land more than anywhere else.

— Clarence Darrow

August 1997, Nashville

At 2:45 a.m. on August 11, 1997, I became aware of just what kind of danger existed in Nashville and every other big city. A sergeant was involved in a long foot chase with a suspect wearing a bulletproof vest and running from a stolen car—none of which, according to all the

people in the public housing community, was a sign he was doing

anything wrong. The two apparently fought for quite a while before

the sergeant became dizzy from Leon Fisher's punches and was forced

to shoot him before Fisher incapacitated him. Fisher already had been

arrested for possession of a firearm, selling narcotics, driving with a

cancelled license, evading arrest, and a string of other offenses dating

to 1993 as a result of constant drug dealing. He also was a suspect in

the June 1997 shooting death of Michael Bradley. But, of course, the

so-called real story, according to the rioters, was the same old tripe:

white cop shot black man for no reason and black man was a good boy

just minding his business. So what did the residents do? Burned down

pretty much everything they could. The *Los Angeles Times* reported the

riot at two hundred to three hundred people and the *New York Times*

wrote the same. There were a lot of people who were really angry at

the police and a lot more who decided it was a good time to get free

stuff. They looted the Dollar General Store. I saw at least fifty looters

amidst the fire. The dollar store was built in an effort to improve the

public housing area, provide jobs to local residents, and make

shopping more convenient for residents. So it made perfect sense to

loot and burn it to the ground.

When I arrived with my new training officer from West Sector, I heard gunshots from many directions and everything I saw, including a couch twenty-five feet in front of me, was on fire. Huge brown dumpsters, located between rows of housing units and filled with cardboard and other debris, were blazing high like candles. Of course, the dollar store was ablaze. We were securing an area to make things relatively safe for the fire department, which had been to this rodeo more than once and weren't coming out of their trucks until they were relatively certain the gunfire from the crowd wasn't directed at them. But, as more police arrived, the group grew even more inflamed. It was a Catch-22 I would experience a lot in the future: people would create unbelievably dangerous situations or commit unthinkable crimes and, when we showed up to stop things from getting worse, blamed us.

If we left, we just encouraged the idiots to do the same thing the next time. If we stayed, we were in for a long bottle-pelting, gunshot-ducking, flaming crap-throwing fun time. Anyway, I didn't know what to do, so I stood there with my shotgun and tried not to look scared out of my mind, which I was. I had to keep looking at different cops to see what they were doing so I knew what I was supposed to do. It seemed like a relatively agreeable line was drawn between us and the crowd, and I was pretty sure we weren't going to

cross it since we were outnumbered by about two hundred people at

the time.

I was trying to figure out what to do if three or four guys

rushed me to kill me. In part, it was an intellectual exercise to keep me

from shitting myself, but I also was seriously trying to figure out what I

would do. Then the idiots started shooting out the streetlights, which

was, I would come to find out, a fairly regular occurrence. My mind

was in overload so I just stood there in a line of cops, watching burning

furniture being thrown off balconies, dumbstruck as to how this was

going to end. I truly didn't have any idea what I was supposed to do.

Have you ever felt really awkward at a party? When you just hang

around the bar and actively think about how to stand and what to do

with your hands? Maybe you pretend-talk on the phone or fake-smile

at someone across the room. You don't know anyone and have no idea

what to do. That's how I felt, only the people at the party, who were

throwing flaming couches and bottles, potentially could shoot me. I

tried to look unconcerned, bored, not aggressive, amused.

In my old Kansas neighborhood, Verona Gardens, a house

caught fire one night. All the residents came out to watch the fire trucks and firefighters working to save what they could of the house. I

was six or seven, the time in every boy's life when a fire truck was the

greatest thing ever, except for an actual real live fire. That had been the

only real fire I'd ever witnessed. So, the incredible scene in front of me

that night was the absolute craziest shit I had ever seen. In my mind, it

was what hell would look like – total chaos, fire everywhere.

Eventually, the crowd just got bored and retreated, having slowly

burned itself out. In the end, the firefighters put out the fires, the

crowd went to bed, and we went back to patrol our areas. I remember

riding back to our sector, past all the still burning dumpsters, watching

the smoke rise, smelling burning trash and smoke, and thinking, *What

the fuck was that?*

My training officer for West Sector was Wilson, an older black

man. He would drive the car from 10:45 p.m., when our shift began,

until about 2 a.m. Then it was my turn to drive while Wilson slept

between calls. I would like to say I learned as much from Wilson as I

did from Jim, but I didn't. Both were similar in their routines: Both

liked to eat early in the shift. Both answered their calls diligently but

weren't for much proactive policing. Both were good at resolving

disputes. But what I learned from Wilson was very important in helping me deal with the population in the projects and ghetto I would

end up policing for the next several years. Wilson had West 24 Zone,

which at the time, was a gold mine of absolute shit. It included two sets

of projects and an area we called "12th and Buck" for 12th Avenue

North and Buchanan Street. At the time, 12th and Buck was a great

place to get into a stolen car chase, get shot at, and respond to

homicide and shots fired calls. Wilson, having about eighteen years on

the force, never went to 12th and Buck, while going there was all I

wanted to do.

Up 12th Avenue was another intersection at Herman Street,

where a car wash was located. A lot of gang members and thugs hung

out at the car wash. The midnight shift didn't have enough officers to

deal with much beyond answering calls and backing up each other on

traffic stops. So the car wash also was a drive-through drug stop for

crack and heroin.

In the parking lot next to the car wash, only after 10 p.m., was a

rusty trailer propped up on cinder blocks. It had metal door which slid

up, along with a small awning. Even by the dim light of the trailer and

surrounding area you could see that any food being sold from the place

was not going to meet a health code with a million dollar bribe attached. But in that trailer was a little, old black man and a fat, old black woman who made the best barbecue pulled pork sandwiches with pickles in the entire South, and therefore, the world. We'd go there almost every night and Wilson would get two sandwiches and I would get one. Thing is, Wilson had to pretend he was ordering three sandwiches because the two old people didn't serve white people, which they made very clear when I tried to order my first one. Now Wilson didn't talk to me much. He'd grunt a command every couple of hours, but that was about it. So I was very unclear as to why we were stopping at this trailer next to the car wash, which was a conspicuous outdoor drug-selling venue. I thought maybe Wilson had a warrant he was going to serve, but the whole area looked way too shady for two cops , one white, to do anything that required exiting our car. That first time, I fell in behind Wilson and figured out we were eating dinner when he ordered his two barbecue sandwiches. I could not believe I was going to eat anything from this trailer. The aroma was amazing, though, and I was hungry and clearly Walter hadn't been poisoned so far. So I decided to order myself a sandwich.

"Hi, ma'am," I said. "A barbecue sandwich with pickles for me, too, please." She snickered.

"We don't serve no white folks," she said. I didn't have an answer for that.

"Hush up and give me a third sandwich," Wilson said. The woman grumbled, but when she gave Wilson his two, she had included a third. He carried the bag to the car and we drove to a safe area in a parking garage to eat. Wilson never offered an explanation, and I didn't ask for one. The message was clear: I was not welcome anywhere near this area, for any reason.

Now, I'd been raised by a Southern father and Southern grandparents with Southern values, but I had not been raised with an ounce of racism. I knew Norma Nan wouldn't buy me a Michael Jackson magazine, but I was too sheltered to understand why. I had a good friend, JASPer, who was black. JASPer was one of my best friends until he went to a private school. My first girlfriend and our best family friends were Jewish. The southern part of Kansas City was white and Christian, but it also was a tolerant place and I didn't judge people by color or religion. I'm sure racism existed there, as it did everywhere, but I don't remember it being overt, and it certainly wasn't a part of my world or childhood. I hadn't seen behavior like this before, from a white or black person, against a white or black person. So I found this blatant racism against me more interesting than offensive.

Not that I even blame the couple for their feelings. They were old and probably had been a victim of some pretty shitty things in the White South during the '50s, '60s, and '70s. They had a right to their beliefs and I certainly wasn't going to be offended by them. I was learning about racism in a different way than most white people did.

In my new area, I noticed other things as well. The black men would try to catch my eye, then spit on the ground. I found that too blatant an aggression to leave unchallenged. But people were smart; they would only do it when they had the numbers behind them to make sure a single cop was incapable of handling them. Later, in the days of the department's FLEX units—uniformed gang and drug units that worked in the projects with the goal of keeping homicides down— we wouldn't tolerate that kind of overt challenge. But at the time I was driving around with Wilson, seeing ghettos and projects for the first time, the constant hatred directed at me for being a cop and being white was eye opening. I was a part of a history I didn't understand in a place I didn't really know.

It was clear these people had been told I was a very bad

character prior to my arrival. These people were doing everything they could to make sure I knew they were my enemy, but I didn't understand why. I was new to this war and unaware we were on different sides. I honestly thought most of the people in the community wanted the police there and that only a few bad eggs were wrecking the neighborhood's peace. That opinion was based on what I thought should be the truth, rather than what I would come to know as the truth: people wanted us to be in the area if they called , but they did not want us actively policing it. I spent two months in West Sector, and the lessons of the barbecue trailer and spitting thugs remained with me.

I had given a pledge to fight for the public, to give my life for another human being, no matter the color of their skin. I took this vow extremely seriously and I didn't understand how these people could possibly be angry with me for being white, or a cop, or the worst possible combination, a white cop. I was willing to die for them! As Billy Joel sings, "Now here you are with your faith, And your Peter Pan advice. You have no scars on your face..." That was me. Poor me. My feelings were hurt by the world. So fucking stupid, but they were.

Chapter 6:

Black Girl Yoda

I once heard a saying that when you're ready, the teacher you need appears before you.

— Emily Byrd Starr

September 1997, Nashville

When I was a boy the Star Wars Trilogy was my Bible. *Star Wars: A New Hope*, *The Empire Strikes Back*, and *Return of the Jedi* were released in 1977, 1980, and 1983, respectively. In 1977, I was three years old, so the characters and story of Darth Vader were a major part

of my play world. I collected all the action figures and made them carry

out epic battles in the bathtub. In the backyard, Darth Vader's Tie

Fighter, held in my right hand, would aggressively pursue Luke

Skywalker's X-Wing Fighter, held in my left hand. Chewbacca and Han

Solo spent months flying the Millennium Falcon around my yard while

chasing Boba Fett in Slave I, his Bounty Hunter ship. My backyard trees

and landscape often morphed into the Ewok home forest planet of

Endor. In winter, my snow-covered yard was the planet Hoth, where

the Rebels were holding back a surprise attack from Darth Vader and

the giant Imperial AT-AT walking machines. Star Wars was and is my

favorite universe, imagined or otherwise. The movies truly were space

operas with good and evil, a princess in distress, a rogue

swashbuckler, a loyal sidekick, a mentor, a wise old master, and the

ultimate villain. *Star Wars* had everything to engage a young idealist's

mind, including the age-old story of the oppressed rising against their

oppressors and slaves throwing off masters. It was the storming of the

Bastille and the shot heard 'round the world at Lexington and Concord

in 1775, all rolled into one, and so much more. I wanted to be a Jedi

Knight capable of using The Force to fight evil more than I ever wanted

anything, and, frankly, I really shouldn't be using past tense.

Good and evil were simple to understand in *Star Wars*. The good guys wore Earth colors – greens, tans, browns —and were human or alien. Bad guys wore colorless, drab, black, dark gray, or white and were mechanized in appearance: they almost always wore a helmet. The good guys were fighting for peace and freedom and shirking off the mantle of tyranny. The Force was a power that could be used by the Sith for evil or the Jedi for good.

To me, Luke Skywalker and the Jedi were the ultimate heroes in the universe, while Darth Vader was clearly the evil villain against which all who were good must fight. Plus, I was being raised in a Christian household in America, so I connected the dots. God represented the Force. Jesus was like Yoda, the wise master training and teaching all of us. Luke was us, capable of great power or great evil, depending on the path we chose or the decisions we make. The devil was obviously Darth Vader: just like Lucifer, Vader was once a good Jedi named Anakin Skywalker, until he turned to the dark side. The good guys fought against tyranny and for freedom while the bad guys, clearly Communists, stood for Soviet Union-type things — whatever those were, but they were definitely evil to a ten-year-old boy in Kansas in 1980. Even when I was four, I was mesmerized by

Star Wars, and like any good father, my dad built me an X-Wing Fighter so I could fly to where Luke Skywalker lived and join him in fighting Darth Vader. Every Saturday morning I would wait and wait for Dad to wake up so we could work on the X-Wing Fighter. I just knew Luke needed my help and I could not for one second allow him to continue the battle against the Empire without my assistance. Dad did a great job. He used some large boards to create a plane-shaped X-Wing and attached an old motor from something, perhaps a lawn mower, to the back.

I was very concerned about firepower, too. Since the Tie Fighters had green laser guns, I needed the red laser guns. Dad found a way. My laser guns were the red reflectors on the small, plastic sticks used as driveway markers in the snow to keep plows from ruining the grass.

"All we have to do," Dad said, "is hook up the reflectors to the laser power source," which, I think, was the same as the former 2 horsepower lawn mower engine.

Dad even built a seat for me on top of one of the boards so I could practice flying until he finished the cockpit, which never quite got done. Dad was in a race to delay the actual flight test of the X-Wing

Fighter until, he hoped, I learned that *Star Wars* wasn't real. My

mother would watch from the window or our deck. Later, she said it

was all rather sad because she knew I wouldn't get to Luke Skywalker

on the power of that X-Wing Fighter. In my imagination, though, I

engaged Darth Vader and the whole Empire in various lightsaber duels

and space battles. On many starry nights, while lying on my back and

looking up at our galaxy, I watched for laser beams that would show

me the direction to aim my X-Wing when I was ready for takeoff.

I never got that X-Wing into space. I never got a lightsaber. I

also found out that being a Jedi was hard. Luke Skywalker had asked

Yoda a lot of the same questions I had for the Academy instructors.

Just as Luke learned about The Force from Yoda while training on

planet Dagobah, I learned about "using force" from instructors while

training in the Academy on planet Nashville.

"How am I to know the good side [of the Force] from the bad?"

Luke asked Yoda.

"You will know when you are calm, at peace, passive," Yoda

replied. "The Jedi use The Force for knowledge and defense, never for attack."

That was a very good piece of advice and it simplified all the policies and legal requirements and conditions of the "use of force" for me. I knew it was wrong to use violence as a Christian and member of a civilized society. I also had no idea how much violence to use to arrest someone. Obviously, one was to use the "minimum amount of force necessary to affect the arrest," but how much was that? In the Academy we would box and wrestle. I hated both. I hated being punched, but who doesn't? Also, I didn't want to hurt anyone. The thought of hurting someone on purpose was a theoretical exercise to me, and I couldn't help but wonder if really hurting someone would make me sad. To me, reason was the mechanism for problem solving as opposed to violence, which was the method of the irrational and thuggish. I wanted to truly find solutions to people's issues much as my father had with psychology. Whereas Dad worked to change a person's behavior, though, I wanted to help bring about justice on the communal level. I was going to be a Jedi and pursue justice with a capital "J"—the Justice of Aristotle, who defined the word as "that which the just man does."

Since just behavior is virtuous behavior, justice encompasses all the other virtues. Virtue is about responding to things under the right circumstances to the appropriate degree. Sometimes this notion is known as Aristotle's Doctrine of the Mean: the ancient sage held the view that moral virtues are states of character lying at the mean between extremes of excess and deficiency. Using the proper level of force to arrest someone (the minimum necessary) would most definitely be the virtuous way to arrest someone, and would, therefore, make me a just police officer. I decided Aristotle's philosophy would be the most virtuous way to police and would therefore be the most just way, since justice includes all virtues. I would strive to be calm, at peace, and passive, reacting justly to all situations, using violence as a last resort and only enough to affect the arrest of a subject.

With that philosophy in mind, after four months on the street with two training officers, I was transferred to the worst area in Nashville with DJ, my new field training officer. DJ was a black woman in her late twenties. She worked in the University Court projects and around a shit part of Nashville called Lafayette Road. Everything I know about policing in a uniform, I learned from two people, and DJ was one of them. She and I were quite the intimidating pair driving around the ghetto — she a five foot four black woman and me a five foot eight white rookie weighing in at one hundred fifty pounds. DJ made it clear very early that she didn't like me and she didn't like Rookies. Further, she thought a white Vanderbilt graduate was not going to last long in her area. DJ considered me worthless. She was not nurturing. I like nurturing. My mom was very nurturing and I had never been considered worthless before. Things between DJ and me didn't improve much when she confirmed that I grew up affluent in the Kansas City suburbs. I don't think DJ could imagine a worse rookie than the one she thought me to be.

She was an incredible cop. She knew her zone, the dope dealers, the gun toters, the gangs. She knew where the crackheads hid, who had warrants on them, what calls were typical bullshit, and what calls could end up in a confrontation. I had never seen crack before so she taught me all about it— how to see if it was real or fake, where crackheads hid crack, where dealers hid crack. She taught me everything I needed to know about arresting someone—all the paperwork, all the charges. She taught me how to fill out affidavits and prepare for trial. Since we spent a great deal of time in court, she taught me how to testify, what tricks criminal defense attorneys use, what charges prosecutors won't prosecute, which judges were good and which were probably crooked and possibly taking money from defense attorneys for lenient sentences. (There was only one and he knows who he is).

DJ was the best mentor I could ever have asked for. She taught me how to speak to the black people in the projects. DJ taught me the real status of race relations in Nashville at the time (not good), and she talked a lot about the real way I needed to talk and act if I wasn't going to be a dead white cop. She wasn't all that nice or respectful to people on the street. In fact, she would downright dog cuss people into the ground, but she taught me how a white, male cop had to act to as opposed to how she, a short, black woman, had to act. She told me what blacks in the ghetto thought of a white cop.

DJ showed me reality on the streets, stripped bare, without the feelings, hopes, desires, wants, needs, and other irrelevant things debated by politicians and academics. She helped make me successful in my career. One last thing about DJ: everyone respected her, though many didn't like her abrasive ways. I loved her to death.

One day, DJ saw a guy she had been after for quite a while. He was tough to catch because he was a fighter and he would run. There were multiple felony warrants on him, including a parole violation. At the time, I didn't think about what a "parole violation" meant. It means you're going back to prison. So when DJ pulled up on the subject, she said, "Get ready for a fight." I was about to ask what "get ready" meant, but I learned quickly. When DJ exited our car and said the guy's name, our subject took two steps and hit her so hard, she was knocked to the ground. As the guy turned toward her again, I hit him with everything I had and tackled him, trying to wrap up his arms, which were swinging wildly at my head. We flipped over a railing and both fell about four feet to the ground. The ground was covered in broken glass, dirt, and litter, like all the ground in all the projects. As we turned into a whirlwind of twirling bodies, I became aware of something very scary: this was the first time I sensed a difference in the goal of someone we were trying to arrest. This guy wasn't fighting to escape; he was fighting to hurt me. As punches rained down on me, I continued to grapple to keep him on the ground until I could come up with a plan.

Meanwhile, my philosopher's brain, with the same level of situational cluelessness as Sheldon from *Big Bang Theory*, is delivering a lecture to my desperate self on the differences between someone fighting to get away and someone fighting to incapacitate you. After

what seemed like eternity but was probably thirty seconds, I was able

to get the guy in a choke hold, which seemed a good start to my

nonexistent plan. I couldn't figure out why our guy suddenly stopped

fighting. I didn't realize DJ was back with us. She had climbed over the

wall where we'd fallen. I was still on my side, my arms around the

guys' neck, his body on top of mine. I felt DJ reach under me and yank

his arm behind his back. She then was able to twist his arm using the

handcuff as a lever until pain forced him to put his other arm behind

his back. Finally, DJ had gotten his hands behind his back enough to

handcuff him.

Once I got to my feet, I realized DJ had just about emptied her

can of OC/CS Freeze +P, which is way worse than pepper spray, into

his face. Her so-called pain compliance measures — read that

"punches"— also helped me finally get the guy under control and into

handcuffs. DJ and I cleaned ourselves up the best we could. Both our

uniforms were covered in grass, blood, and of course, the lovely Chanel

No. 5 scent of the OC/CS spray that burned our nostrils and reddened

our eyes. We tried to straighten each other up, too—clean up cuts and

blood from our arms, knees, elbows, faces, and heads, but it was apparent both our uniforms were beyond salvation. DJ had a black eye

and swollen face, and I was covered in dirt, blood, cuts, and bruises.

But that was the day I earned DJ's respect. It was an important

achievement for me.

This interaction was going to need some analysis, I thought. As I

looked at DJ's face, I couldn't help but question the nature of

confrontations and how a Jedi should handle them. Certainly, this was

beyond the scope of my Christian education. Cops can't turn the other

cheek, especially when the first cheek shot knocks you down. I was not

calm, at peace, or passive. That was the first time I had become really

violent. I wasn't sure anymore about waiting until the suspect attacked

before we attacked. Somehow, that seemed stupid. This confrontation

also left a new emotion burning in my soul — hate.

Chapter 7:

Lights! Camera!

Bad Boys, Bad Boys, Whatcha gonna do?
Whatcha gonna do when they come for you?

— Bad Boys, "Inner Circle"

September 1997, Nashville

For the last two weeks of my training period in Central Sector

with DJ, guess who came to town? *COPS*, the landmark reality show

that began in March 1989. In the early '90s, everyone watched *COPS*. It aired its 850th episode in the 2012-2013 season. DJ was off, and I was paired with another officer named Eric. He and I were pretty good at getting into trouble so they had the two *COPS* guys — a cameraman and a sound mixer — ride with us for approximately two weeks. The *COPS* crew adopts a fly-on-the-wall approach when filming. You'd be surprised how many people ignore them. My theory is that so many of the people in the ghetto use the police to solve their problems—from domestic and civil property issues to money and parenting issues— that they're used to having the police officers involved in their lives. Lots of people would view having police officers at their house as an embarrassing or dramatic situation, but people in the inner city just see them as part of their environment or a service to use. So if two more guys with a camera, dressed in black gear show up, who cares? Obviously, if the footage has a chance to be used, the participants are asked to sign a waiver form and, surprisingly, they do.

I was amazed to actually have *COPS* riding with us and, frankly, their presence fed into my "this is just a big game" mentality. I was going to be on TV! Truth be told, *COPS*, the police chief, and the mayor do have some ground rules for filming. The *COPS* guys said they have a ton of footage of police chasing guys through the projects and asked us to be creative and respond to as many unique or drama-filled incidents as possible. The chief and mayor got to veto what was aired. Since Nashville, known as the country music capital of the world, is a major tourist town, neither the chief nor the mayor wanted crime filmed in the famous Nashville Downtown area, which makes good sense. So we were on the lookout for interesting things that didn't happen downtown and didn't feature guys being chased through the projects. Guess what we ended up doing most of the time? Yep. Chasing guys through the downtown area or the projects. Oh, well. But we did get our footage. We certainly did.

COPS Season 10, Episode 33, became known as "The Dog Man Episode." Eric and I responded to a stolen vehicle in progress call near the Settle Court projects. We arrived to see an officer fighting in the street with a male subject who broke away and ran diagonally toward our car. The officer yelled over the radio that the subject had a gun. I jumped out the passenger side of our car and chased him on foot while Eric slammed the car into reverse and the COPS crew filmed out the rear window. I was unfamiliar with those projects and took a wrong turn. One of the annoying things about the projects is that when one bad guy comes tearing through, a crowd of males run, too, to hide their dope or guns. You have to focus on the guy you're chasing. Otherwise, you're like a dog who just ran into a flock of geese.

As I ran, I gambled that I if I went left, around the building in front of me, the suspect would go right, see Eric and the *COPS* crew running at him from the far right side of the building, and then have to circle back around toward me. It worked: we just about ran into each other as we both came around the corner of another building, two rows from where the Eric and the COPS crew were flushing him in my direction. I can't say who was more surprised when we almost collided. I knocked him down and drew my gun just as Eric arrived with the others and handcuffed him. We found his gun next to him on the grass where he must have dropped or thrown it when we almost ran into each other.

The best part of the story is that a stray dog wandered over to us just as the suspect was talking and ending every sentence with "man": "I didn't have no gun, man." "I didn't steal no car, man." " You just harassing me, man." The stray dog sniffed his face, to which he said, "Come on, dog, man! He dog, man! Get away dog, man." That's how he became the "Dog Man" and wound up in jail while Eric and I wound up on TV. Of course, I had rehearsed a classic line for the fade to black moment at the end. "You can run from the police," I said, "but you will just go to jail tired". Cheesy. I know.

Of course, having the *COPS* crew ride with us only reinforced my belief that I was in a wonderful game in which I was playing the hero. Sure, danger existed, but I was triumphing over evil and always would. Not soon after this incident, I ended up in a foot chase that should have qualified me for the Nashville Marathon. As I turned the corner with DJ one afternoon while walking through the projects, we spied Eric and the *COPS* crew sneaking around the opposite corner of the building. Eric's voice came over the radio in a hushed tone, "DJ. That guy about to come out of the apartment is armed and is robbing it." Dispatch quickly chimed in, "All cars, clear the air for 423B (Eric)."

The guy came out, saw DJ and me, and took off, gun in hand. Eric and DJ drew their guns and yelled for the suspect to get on the ground. The *COPS* camera guys quickly took cover by the building in case there was gunfire. Everyone had seen the danger but the rookie— me. I was running blindly after him. The suspect didn't look up for about thirty seconds after his sprint took him several blocks away. When he did, he saw me ten yards away and continued to run, gripping the gun with his right hand and turning his head slightly to look back at me over his left shoulder, as if deciding whether to stop and square

up. We ran for another forty-five seconds or so. At almost a quarter-

mile from where we'd started, we twisted and turned through

playgrounds, a small park, buildings, parking lots, and intersections. I

was reveling in the chase. There was no chance this thug was going to

outrun me. I loved the sound of his breathing getting labored and I

knew I'd have him in another sixty seconds. He was able to keep

distance between us because I had to swing wide when turning

corners to make sure he didn't duck behind and ambush me when I

came around a bend. *DJ and Eric would be so impressed*, I thought. I was

almost smiling as I thought about what a good "Atta Boy" I'd get at roll

call the next morning in front of the other veteran officers. Plus, I knew

this would get back to the other guys and girls in my Session 32 Class

and they'd be proud of me, too, and it'd be a nice mark for our class, as

a whole. Not to mention, this scene would be a phenomenal episode

for *COPS*! I was certain they were still behind me, filming my every

stride.

As the suspect and I came up on a major intersection, Lafayette

and University Court projects, I was planning my diving tackle. It

would be the shot of the year on *COPS*. I was still oblivious, though, to the fact the suspect was carrying a gun. It was a small .38, but, sadly, I

wasn't looking at his hands. I was focused on how thrilling the chase

was, how I had outlasted everyone, and how in a hundred yards or

more, this guy was going to get a primo flying tackle just as we were

going to hit the small parking lot of a convenience store at the

intersection. It was then I heard DJ's voice on the radio yell, "Someone,

get with my rookie! He's chasing that armed 10-52 suspect on foot

toward University Court!"

The blood drained from my face. The fun was gone. 10-52

meant "shooting." The suspect had just shot someone in that

apartment just prior to our arrival. He still had the gun. He also had

nothing to lose. He'd probably try to shoot me to end this chase. When

I stopped thinking about my own glory and focused on his right hand, I

saw the silver handgun. He had been canting himself, deciding whether

to turn and shoot me the whole time, not checking to see how close I

was to him. It was then we hit the small parking lot. At the same time,

three police cars slammed into the lot, half blocking the intersection.

DJ, Eric, and another cop jumped out with shotguns and blocked our

path.

"Drop the gun!" they yelled. "Get the fuck on the ground!"

Knowing he was caught, the suspect dropped the gun even before the commands had been finished. He laid himself out prone and Eric ran to handcuff him.

DJ slung her shotgun, walked up to me, shoved me hard in the chest with her left hand, and yelled, "What the fuck were you doing, rookie!? What the fuck are you doing, you goddamn rookie idiot fuck!? You don't chase people through here by your white fucking self and without giving directions on the radio! You don't outrun your help and then stay silent on the radio and you don't chase armed suspects ten fucking yards behind where they can shoot you when they turn around. You don't chase armed shitbags with your gun in your holster, either! God, you're a dumb fuck!" Then she turned around and walked toward the suspect to start dealing with him.

Eric came up to me, as did another officer. "Dude," Eric said, in a much quieter voice. "What the fuck? You could have been killed very easily. This isn't a game, dude. They will shoot you."

So much for my vision of greatness and glory. DJ was right: this whole scene had been a game to me — a race like the one in fourth grade where I'd won the second-place ribbon. My buddy Steve always won the first-place ribbons, but I'd been fast that day and had taken second, right behind him with a strong push at the end of the fifty-yard dash. I had worn my tube socks pulled up to reduce friction and my lucky blue and red striped shirt. I took first that day on the team relay: Steve was on my relay team. I'd been envisioning this race much the same—blue ribbon, red ribbon, Ribbons for Ryan! The *COPS* guys had never even turned the cameras back on after the suspect and I had sprinted off. Intellectually, I understood I was in a dangerous situation, but, on another level, I understood I was going to be on TV and this was a fantastic game. I can't say my feelings weren't hurt. They were. But quickly, very quickly, I would learn these things the hard way. DJ's loud anger and Eric's quieter reprimand had come from hundreds of scars that would soon burn through me—the hard way, too.

The *COPS* "Dog Man" episode was aired June 27, 1998. By then, I'd been in several awful incidents, including a shooting, and was having horrible nightly nightmares. By then, I was well aware the "game" had ended. In those eight months, I went from Rookie Ryan to someone my mother described, through tears, as "cold and gone." I sat and watched the episode with a beer on a vacation by myself with the bartender. He said it was "OK." He'd seen more exciting ones.

Chapter 8:

Gilligan and The

Skipper

One of the most beautiful qualities of true friendship is to understand and to be understood.

— Lucius Annaeus Seneca

October 1997, Nashville

Randy Allen sat behind me in the Academy and he and I

became fast friends. We both liked cartoons, video games, and had similar family backgrounds. Randy's dad was a medical doctor, so he also had grown up in an affluent house neighborhood. We had similar views on the world, too. He loved knives, guns, and explosives. This was the perfect job for Randy, who was also an emergency medical technician and had worked on an ambulance. The instructors never picked on Randy very much. He was always neatly kept, got good grades, wasn't too loud, marched just fine, never finished first in running but never finished last, excelled at the medical training, and was, if not the best shot, then the second best shot with either the Glock 22 .40-caliber pistol and Remington 870 shotgun with which we were trained. Randy was bigger than me—five foot ten and fairly large at two hundred thirty pounds. He called me "Little Buddy," which is what the Skipper called Gilligan. We even looked like that famous duo from *Gilligan's Island* when we were together.

Randy and I ended up living together in a house we rented in South Nashville. The first six months we were living together required each of us to respect the other guy's sleep schedule. We were on two-month shifts during our Sector Rotational Period. The first two months, I worked 3 p.m. to 11 p.m. with Jim in South Sector and Randy worked 11 p.m. to 7 p.m. in West Sector. Then, in July and August, I

was working 11 p.m. to 7 a.m. in West Sector and Randy was working

7 a.m. to 3 p.m. in Central Sector. You throw in court appearances at

9:15 a.m. and 10:45 a.m. if you made an arrest the night before, and

someone was always sleeping, waking up, or going to bed in our house.

We hardly saw each other the whole six months.

For a while in the last two months, Randy and I both worked

the 11 p.m. to 7 a.m. shift. I thought of myself as Batman during this

time, sleeping during the day and fighting crime at night. I put a black

pirate flag on the wall to cover my windows and keep the light out, so I

could sleep. Randy and I would both get home about 7:30 a.m., pop

open beers, and watch *Bugs Bunny* or play video games while drinking.

Morning was our night. We kept our police radio on the whole time

because we didn't want to miss anything exciting. We would have

worked for free back then. The curtain had been pulled back from the

world we thought we knew. Or perhaps a transparency had been laid

over the world, revealing all the true things going on. We couldn't

drive to the store without looking for criminals on the way.

Randy and I had long conversations about the concept and

obligation of the legal phrase "duty to act." We both believed that we, as the sacred guardians of justice, defenders of the land, and thwarters

of evil, always had a duty to act. We decided we would act in the face of

any danger and that Randy, I, and all police, when off duty, should be

obligated not just to be good observers but to be prepared to fight at

any moment. We decided there was no "off duty," that Justice herself

had not bestowed this privilege, this honor, to fight as God's very own

sword at her side and in her name, if she had not meant for us to be

vigilant and prepared every moment of every day.

Randy and I loved to swap stories, and if we heard the other

guy answer the radio for a call, we were both excited to hear the

outcome. I don't remember worrying for Randy, and I don't think he

worried for me. That came later. At the time, Randy and I just assumed

the outcome would be either a good or boring story, but nothing more

or less. We had a slight competition going as well. Randy got to see the

first suicide. I got to be in the first pursuit. Randy got to drive a police

car first. (Jim let me drive once in all of April, May, and June, and he

made the experience so miserable that I begged him to drive again

after two hours). Those times we had the same night off, we'd go to

O'Charley's in Brentwood. There was a bartender there, Donna, we

both thought was good-looking, and we'd argue for days about which of us she liked better. (Turns out, neither, despite years of trying on

both our parts). We'd tell our day's stories for hours over beers and

burgers. It wasn't brandy and cigars. We knew we weren't ruling the

universe. But we were happy and proud of ourselves for being on our

way to being good cops and starting, so very slowly, to handle

situations like our training officers did.

In those days, we were like sponges, soaking up every

magazine and book we could read. Randy was a big gun guy, which I

never was. He was always buying new knives or some new light for his

shotgun, or a laser sight for his backup gun. We felt like superheroes

and we believed we were truly helping the world. I was dating a

beautiful girl named Susan at the time and Randy was dating one of

her friends, Jenny. We went to concerts together, had cookouts,

watched movies. Life was good.

The biggest competition we would have admitted to having

was over who'd get a take-home car first. Nashville allowed its officers

to bring their cars home if they lived in Davidson County. It was good

for the public to see police cars in neighborhoods and not just at the

police station, and the practice prevented wear and tear on vehicles

that otherwise would have been used twenty-four hours a day as they were passed off, shift to shift. The take-home car was the golden prize

to a rookie. Your very own Batmobile! I can't really say who won this

race: I was given my take-home car before Randy by about two

months. My car, however, was a big box 1991 Ford LTD. When Randy

got his car, it was a really cool 1996 Crown Victoria with the new body

style. A year later, though, I got the 1999 Crown Vic with the brand

new body style. Then he got the same one like a month later. *Argh!* I

guess it was a tie.

Too bad more people couldn't have seen us back then, because

we thought we were the shit. We would keep on our portable radios—

mine on West, his on South—so we could hear what was happening in

our sectors when we were forced to take days off. I can see how people

get addicted to listening to police scanners. The phenomenon must be

the same for astronomers when they look into the night sky with a

giant telescope and are gobsmacked by what they can't see with the

naked eye. When you listen to a police radio, you are listening to

constant chaos all around you, a chaos most people never see. Turning

the radio off was unthinkable for the first year or so. Eventually, we

realized we were just sticking our fingers in the dike, just like the Little

Dutch Boy, and we turned off the radio.

One of the hardest things during the first year you are a cop in a city is the constant bombardment of new experiences. The biggest gap between a rookie and a veteran is knowing what to do, what to say, and, most importantly, what was about to happen next. All of those skills are learned through experience. Randy and I, along with the brethren from MNPD Class Session 32—"With Discipline and Pride our Blood runs Blue, Together as One, We're Session 32"—were learning and growing. Some were failing, but most were growing into the next additions to the Thin Blue Line. Randy liked South Nashville, where he was ultimately assigned. South Sector didn't have the same horribleness of the projects with their constant homicides and robberies, but it was much busier. Where I worked, you arrest someone for something whenever you wanted. It was the fish in a barrel metaphor. But in South Sector, it was call to call to call for the whole shift. Oftentimes when Randy's shift checked in, they would be twenty to thirty calls behind already and would go balls to the wall until they checked out. The old West Sector 20s Zones could be quiet because criminals don't call the police on other criminals all that much, but we had as much work as we wanted because they kept shooting each other.

Randy and I would always meet after work to swap our stories at the local O'Charley's. I had taken to wearing a cowboy hat with my boots. Yes, perhaps I was still playing dress up, but I was also sending the world a message in my own way. I wore a white straw Stetson for a while. Eventually, it got beat up, so I switched to a black one.

I loved Randy like a brother. He was an excellent cop. I just think he never understood how much they hated us in the projects. Randy didn't hate anyone. He always had a smile on his face, always believed that, if he was nice to you, you wouldn't have a reason to hate him. He thought if he gave respect, he would get it, and he would come for you over any hill, through any door.

We got to work together for a brief stint on the West Sector FLEX unit about four years into the job. My favorite story about Randy began with a dispatch call stating a member of the 12th Street Gang was in the dead end of the horseshoe in the John Henry Hale projects. Now, you didn't want to drive down the dead end of the horseshoe at night by yourself for a million reasons, one being that there a lot of people at the dead end with guns, and those people didn't care for us boys in blue. In addition, at the time, I was a member of West FLEX Gangs/Drugs Task Force. They knew our names, car numbers, and when we worked. They also knew we wouldn't drive by them. They

called us the "Jump Out Boys," for obvious reasons, and we were proud

of that nickname , though it meant we had to live up to the reputation.

Living up to the reputation of someone who would do dangerous

things to catch dangerous people made those dangerous people

nervous and more dangerous. The whole thing became a self-fulfilling

prophecy of violence. They knew we were going to come for them, and

they made sure they were prepared.

So I wasn't anonymous when I pulled my car through the

horseshoe — something we liked to do just to see who would run.

Usually, we rode in pairs, for protection, but that night I was alone

because we were short. Randy, who was new to the unit, also was

riding alone. The call said the armed suspect was wearing an orange

Tennessee Vols jacket: he wasn't exactly seeking anonymity. Lo and

behold, just as I made the U-turn from the horseshoe, there he was,

standing on the sidewalk. My first thought was, *I don't want to die

tonight*. My first vision was of him turning around and shooting me as I

approached. But who am I? Am I the man who walks away in fear? Am

I the cop who drives by, radios "I don't see him, must have left the

area," and drives back to safety? Do I have any good reason to approach this guy near midnight in the middle of the projects? Who

would he shoot, anyway? Another drug dealer? So what? But those

aren't the right questions. The correct question is: "Will I allow my fear

to win?"

My answer always was a painful, thoughtful, gut-wrenching,

"No, Never." So I grabbed the microphone, quickly said, "Frank One

Forty-Four , I have the 10-54 Subject dead end of the horseshoe,

orange jacket, start another car now!" Then I threw the car in park,

jumped out, took a couple of steps toward him, drew my gun, and

ordered his hands over his head. Much to my shock, he complied. As he

lifted his hands, his jacket pulled up and two things happened at the

same time: I saw the gun tucked into the waistband of his pants. He

realized I saw the gun. What I didn't know was that he had an eight-

year parole violation against him, meaning that if he was arrested, he

was going back to prison for eight years, in addition to whatever the

new charges and verdicts added on to his sentence. Fortunately or

unfortunately, I had closed the distance between us and stood a couple

of feet away. His hands remained near his head. He was much, much

taller than my five-foot-eight frame, which meant that, to handcuff

him, I couldn't grab his hands without throwing myself off balance. Yet

I also couldn't have him put his hands behind his back because that's

where the gun was.

As I ordered him to his knees, I grabbed for his waistband with

my right hand to snatch his gun. That's when he spun to the right and

grabbed my wrist. I was in trouble. I reached my left arm around his

neck, spun to the right as he did, and pulled the front of my body into

the back of his. There we were: I had one hand on his gun, and he had a

hold of that wrist. I had my other hand wrapped around his neck. I was

holding a spinning bear that was trying to rip me off him and I didn't

have a solution. So I held on, adrenaline and fear slamming into me,

knowing if he ripped me off, I would be in a Old-West-High Noon on

Main Street draw with a guy who was much stronger and taller than I

was. My only chance was help coming. But we weren't in a good place

for a cop to see. There was no light down at the dead end of the

horseshoe. Most of the lights attached to the public housing had been

shot out or hit with rocks. We struggled as he tried to pull free of the

arm I had around his neck while I kept the other on his gun and

strained to keep us tied up together. I was deciding if I could

disengage, draw, and shoot him before he could spin and shoot me. I

was running out of time when, suddenly, I was in the air, off my feet, and slamming forward into the suspect, who was slamming, facedown,

onto the concrete street. I heard Randy's voice, "I will fucking kill you!"

As he crashed down, the suspect released my wrist. I yanked the gun

out of his waistband, rolled away, and drew my own gun on him. But

there was Big Randy, angry as a bull, yanking the guy into handcuffs.

Randy had found me and had come to save his Little Buddy. His car

was on the grass, where he'd just driven straight through some

laundry lines and around the glass-covered playground to come

directly to where he thought I'd be. He'd been right. Randy had come

from behind and picked us up like a crazy linebacker sacking two

quarterbacks and flattened us both, pinning the suspect under me.

Randy and I had to go to O'Charley's again that night. They had

been listening to us for years and this story was going to be a crowd-

pleaser. I arrived around midnight, later than Randy. We were in street

clothes, and I regaled them with Randy's performance, even raging, "I

will fucking kill you," as he did before pile driving us. All that fear and

hate and anger already had become just another story to be told to

demonstrate who we were, down deep. A Scottish philosopher I read

at Vanderbilt, Alasdair MacIntyre, once made the point that we're all

just a sum of the narratives we tell about ourselves, plus the stories others tell about us. I remember telling that story a lot. Randy loved it.

He liked the part about his swooping in to save me. He wouldn't tell

you he hated those people—criminals, or whatever you want to call

them. He didn't like them. He loved to arrest them and be a part of the

foot chases and tackles, car pursuits, and search warrants.

But I don't think they had hurt him yet. You see, all that

changes once they hurt you. Maybe one guy almost kills you. Maybe

they kill a friend of yours—a good cop with a family. Maybe they

destroy what you believe about people, society, religion, your world.

Then you have to take that fear and turn it into aggression. In order to

survive, you have to learn to hate them and treat them like scorpions.

You have to *know*, to truly *know*, they will bite you if you get at all

close. You have to shut down everything, or one thing can get in. You

can't let that one thing get inside you. A single drop of water will start

the dam breaking. I don't think Randy realized that some people are

evil and don't need a reason to kill. Not until August 2005.

Chapter 9:

Learning to Hurt

Democracy don't rule the world. You'd better get that in your head; This world is ruled by violence, But I guess that's better left unsaid.

—Bob Dylan, "Union Sundown"

October 1997, Nashville

After I left roll call on October 1, 1997, I drove my own police car by myself, with no training wheels. When I pulled out of the station, I actually whooped out loud, I was so excited and proud. I was going to drive fast in my own police car and turn the lights and siren

on by myself. What little boy hasn't dreamed of that day? I was

assigned to 24 Zone as 24B1, which meant I was an extra car in the

small but shitty and dangerous area we simply referred to as "18th and

Buchanan." After six months in the Academy and another six riding

with three different field training officers, I really thought I knew what

I was doing out on the street. Just like a teenager who truly believes he

has things figured out, I was pretty sure I was about to restore justice

to the world. In fact, having just left DJ as my last field training officer,

and having just found out what crack cocaine looks like and where it

can be located, I decided to investigate my 24 Zone to find some. I was

on the lookout for suspicious behavior, which I hoped I would

recognize. I was still not very sure what suspicious behavior actually

was. But I was on the lookout and a force to be reckoned with. I quickly

spied a young male engaged in what I believed to be suspicious

behavior. So I pulled up and began to show him my sly cop talk so as to

elicit all his secrets and force him to confess his crimes.

"Hey, man, what's your name?" I asked.

"Why?" Professor Moriarty replied to my Sherlock Holmes.

"What are you doing just hanging out on this corner?" I was tightening my trap!

"What the fuck you think, man? Waiting for the bus," said my subject, pointing at the bus stop sign I'd missed. *Way to go, Sherlock*, I thought.

"OK, good," I said. "Have a nice day." I quickly got back in my police car and left, vowing to learn a lot more about where I was and what suspicious behavior looked like before I made an ass of myself again.

Two weeks later, I had a good handle on the area for which I was responsible. It was about as bad as an area can get, but I was having a lot of fun problem solving different situations. I was determined to leave everyone better than I found him or her, if at all possible. I was enjoying playing Solomon. In my mind, I was making a massive difference in people's lives and I believed I was solving issues instead of, as the more experienced cops said, delaying their inevitable result. Turns out, I was wrong.

I remember being especially pleased with myself one day on a call at a convenience store called Circle K, which was a source of a million problems. If it wasn't getting robbed, it was getting looted. If it wasn't getting looted, people were getting shot in the alley behind it. If people weren't getting shot in the alley behind it, people were smoking crack in the parking lot, and on and on. Anyway, the store clerk called 911 and said a very large man was threatening to kill her. While that sounds serious, and sometimes was serious, a lot of calls in and around the projects started that way because people knew the call would be prioritized and we'd come running. I arrived at the Circle K and spoke with the clerk.

"Hi," I said. "You called the police?"

"Yeah, see that big-ass nigger in the back?" the clerk asked. (Black people in the ghetto had no problem with the word "nigger" when talking about each other, but we knew goddamn well to never get within ten miles of that word. AT&T and Verizon have nothing on the ghetto rumor network. If you didn't want to get shot while walking through the projects, it was important to develop a "good" reputation as someone who was fair, respectful, and consistent. It also was a goal of my white-cop ass not to get shot in the back. So I never responded to the "N" word, ever.)

"Yeah, I see the man," I said. "What happened?"

"He came in here all acting a fool," she informed me. "He was cussin' and sayin' shit, talkin' 'bout how he ain't afraid of nothin' and was gonna do what he want and kill me if I said anything."

"What did you say when he walked in? Did you say something about him being here? Do you know him?" I asked, having learned that the stories police are told usually start in the middle, where the "victim" was offended.

"Yeah, I know him," she said. "He comes around here acting up all the time and y'all lock him up sometimes 'cause he's crazy."

"OK. Well, what do you want? You want him arrested for trespassing or just to leave?" I asked. Most stores in and around the ghetto file trespassing waivers with their local police precinct. The waivers give police permission to prosecute trespassers without consent from the owner or management. That prevents crackheads from smoking behind the store or homeless people from panhandling outside the doors, which keeps customers away. Because trespassing is a misdemeanor, the victim must prosecute. The victim is the store. Clerks are not responsible for the legal prosecution for every crime against the store. If they were, some, like this one, would be in court all

the time.

"Just tell him to leave and he can't come back anymore," she

requested.

"OK", I said, turning to walk to the back of the store where the

suspect was standing and pretending to shop.

"How you doing today?" I asked, confronting the subject. The

clerk was right. He was big, about six foot two, three hundred pounds.

"I just want buy stuff," he replied, "and that bitch won't let me."

"Yeah, that's what she said," I replied. "Did you say something

to her? She says you threatened her."

"She don't own the store," he said, beginning to get louder. "I

can come here if I want and I ain't leaving." This was not going well.

Different tact.

"Look, partner, she is being unfair to you, but she is the clerk

and while she is working, she can tell you to leave. That's the law. You

have to leave. But look, I think you should leave," I reasoned, "because

you shouldn't give your money to her store. If she is going to treat you like this, you should leave and go somewhere else and spend your money.

"You ain't a millionaire, right?" I continued. "You only have so much money and you shouldn't give any of it to her store."

"She can't tell me what to do," he countered, angrily.

"She's not telling you what to do. You don't want to give her your money 'cause she's rude," I said. "Where do you want to go? I will take you there personally. Where do you want to go?" I just wanted to get him away from the store because I had a feeling that if I left, I would be called back in three minutes.

"I don't want to go nowhere else," the subject said. "I will just leave because I want to leave." He started walking to the front of the store.

"OK, sounds good to me," I said. "I will go with you and we will leave the store. You don't want to give her your money, anyway." Much relieved, and proud of myself for diffusing the situation, I walked with my guy to the front. But I had to make sure that I wouldn't be called back and that the guy knew that he was banned from the store — at least for that day. This part was always touchy.

"Look, partner, you can't come back in here today, do you understand?" I said.

"I know you are leaving because you want to leave. You are a good man, but she will just call us again if you come back, OK?"

"I don't want him in the parking lot, either," the clerk said. "He yells at the people and harasses everyone."

"OK, he knows that." I said. "You know that. No parking lot either, right? You are going to take your hard-earned money to some other store that appreciates you, right?" I took a deep breath. "If you come back here today, I'm going to have to arrest you for trespassing, OK? So don't let her get to you. You just go wherever you want, but not here. Sound good?"

"Sounds good to me." the guy agreed. We walked out of the store together.

"Have a good day," I said, heading back into the store. Inside, I told the clerk to call us if he came back. She said she would. I was feeling proud of myself that I'd handled a very tense situation by myself and was able to work it out to everyone's satisfaction. I opened

the door to the store, and walked outside to find my guy sitting on the

curb five feet from the front door. Not good.

"OK, let's go," I said. "We agreed you would go. Now come on,

you have to leave. You don't want to go to jail for trespassing, so you

need to go."

He stood, as if to go, turned toward me, and yelled, "Fuck you. I

ain't going."

"Fine," I said. "Now you are going to jail." I grabbed his left arm.

When I did, he swung with his right and punched me in the head. I

ducked enough (and was shorter than him by enough) that he struck

only the side of the face. I staggered, held his left wrist with both my

hands, and tried to spin him to the ground. But it was useless. He was

so much bigger than I was. He swung wildly at my head as I kept trying

to spin him around and spin myself out of the range of his blows. I

didn't want to release him because I didn't know how I'd ever get near

him again. But he seemed impossible to move: he was so thick and was

six inches taller. He landed another punch to the side of my head. I

decided the plan wasn't working and I'd use my new OC/CS pepper spray. I knew what this spray did. I'd been sprayed in the face and eyes

with it in the Academy. It incapacitated me. I had seen DJ spray the guy

we fought in the University Court projects. He couldn't continue

fighting. Hell, DJ and I were gagging and choking from the secondary

spray. So I was confident in my next move.

Using my right hand, I unholstered the spray. I pulled him

toward me with my left hand, which still had a hold of his left wrist. As

he drew closer, I unloaded the spray into his face. I thought I soaked

him pretty good, so I was stunned when he yanked his left hand from

my grip, wiped his face with both hands, and punched me on the top of

the head as I ducked.

I had no doubt that I'd missed him. That could be the only

explanation. So I sprayed him again—a lot, right in the face and eyes.

He continued to come at me, not even stopping to wipe his face that

time. Fury flashed in his eyes.

"I'm going to kill you!" he yelled. "Going to kill you! AGGGGG!!" I

backed off and went through my training in my mind: hands, spray,

baton. I yanked out my metal ASP and snapped out all thirty-two

inches.

"Put your hands behind your back!" I shouted. "Stop resisting!" I hit him as hard as I could on his arm. He didn't stop coming. He just kept coming. "Put your hands behind your back! Put your hands behind your back! Put your hands behind your back!"

Every time he tried to punch me, I hit him as hard as I could. I ducked under a punch and hit him in the knees. Nothing. I hit his left hand near the wrist as he punched me in the side of my head with his right fist. I heard the bones in his hand and wrist crack and kept screaming, "Put your hands behind your back!" Finally, I realized he was beyond feeling pain. I wasn't. I was dizzy from being hit so many times and yelling. As he punched me again, I felt my skin rip open near my eyebrow and blood pour down my cheek.

I hit him in the face as hard as I could with my metal baton. I knew that was deadly force, technically, but I had to try something. I watched his bottom lip rip, and slowly, like a slug, fall off and hit the ground. I was beating another human being to death and I wanted to throw up. While I was dumbstruck at my own actions, he punched me again. I didn't know what to do, and then I remembered: The radio, the calvary. They had taught us in the Academy that you could key the radio and talk over a dispatcher, but not other cops. Even though the other cops couldn't hear you because the dispatcher is talking, the

dispatcher can hear you. I waited a couple of seconds as my hearing

returned from the effects of my adrenaline, and I heard her voice, her

angel voice.

"Unit 124, get me some cars! Get me some cars! Help!" I yelled

as I kept swinging my baton. I heard her pause in her directions to the

other cops and then there were the glorious three beeps before she

said, "Attention all cars, 124B code 5000 at 28th and Jefferson. Officer

yelling for help, Circle K at 28th and Jefferson. All cars in the area,

respond. Code 3."

Over my radio, I heard, "22 in route," "23 in route," "12 in

route," "31 in route," "25 in route," "Central 27 in route," "West 15 in

route." When I heard Randy's voice come over — "South 21 in route"

— I wanted to cry. I knew if I could hang on, I would make it. I swung

and I swung and I swung. There was blood everywhere when I heard

the sirens. I saw blue lights and cops jumping from cars and running

toward us, and I felt very tired and very sad.

Five cops sprayed Larry Charles before tackling him to the

ground and putting him into handcuffs. My sergeant and several other guys informed me that, two years earlier, Charles had tried to chop down the telephone pole in front of the store with an ax. He had to be subdued by five or six officers and was taken to a mental institution where he had remained until recently.

DJ was there, patting me on the shoulder and saying, "Good job, rookie." Then she laughed and left. Several more cops came up to me and said, "Way to go! That's awesome. Well done!" I was confused. I was getting praise and admiration, but I felt so very sad. I had never hurt someone so badly. I had never hurt anyone. I didn't want to hurt anyone. Then I realized why they were congratulating me. For one thing, they were focused solely on the end result and never thought about the means. They dismissed the means as always justifiable to the end of – not justice, not right, not morality, not good — but survival. The emotion in their voices was not admiration for me but hate for Larry Charles.

Ambulances were called and my guy, Larry Charles, had to go to the hospital for a lot of stitches, a broken arm and wrist, and a cracked jaw. He needed a new bottom lip, too. I got some stitches and went home. Then I drank beer until I passed out so I wouldn't dream.

There was a blacksmith inside my head, pounding, shaping, and working everything that I used to think and believe into walls to keep out everything I was learning and feeling. I was truly a new man. And deep down, I knew I hated that new man.

Chapter 10:

Because You

Deserve You

No one is born hating others.

— Daisaku Ikeda

November 1997, Nashville

Once, I was called to a 10-41PE, which is a domestic violence

incident, in progress, emergency. I was around the corner and responded within thirty seconds. As I exited my police car, a woman in a nearby public housing unit yelled, "You better get in there before he kills her!" As I approached the house I heard glass crashing and screaming, I saw into the apartment, which looked like it'd been hit with a tornado. Furniture was knocked over. A smashed mirror was on the floor and broken glass was everywhere. There was a brief moment I brought to mind that instant when the flame on a cigarette lighter blinks out and you think you blew it out. Actually, though, it's out for just a second. I felt the boy inside me fold into a small ball and a pit in my stomach ignited. I felt loss and sadness. I felt afraid of the future and for my life. Then a flame danced inside me and the wolf was there. The boy was thrown away, again.

I slammed my baton into the outer glass door, knocked away what glass I could, and threw myself through the rest of the shards and into the room. The screaming continued as I made my way down the hall, gun drawn, to its source. When I looked around the corner, I saw a man trying to cut the nipple out of a woman's breast. As I raised my gun to shoot him, he dropped the knife and fell, backward, off the bed and onto the floor. That saved his life. I couldn't shoot him without his knife and he knew it. He jumped at me, and holstering my Glock, I wrestled with him, smashing us both into a dresser with a mirror. He spun away and grabbed a lamp, swinging it at my head. I ducked and lifted my arm, suffering a large bruise and cut as it smashed into my bicep and elbow. The explosion of violence in my head was like a firecracker — a quick, short CRACK! The rage inside me came from a place the other violent man just couldn't go. Winning was the point, and winning did not mean living. It meant delivering greater violence, not caring about the outcome, enjoying the sick crying of the little boy inside. Winning was coming at another who had chosen violence with such soulless blackness that he couldn't ever hope to match.

I dove into the man and knocked him down, both of us tripping over a nightstand. He tried to rise. I was quicker. I spun him and drove him toward the dresser, slamming his head into the mirror again and again until he stopped fighting, at which point I slammed him down into the cheap wood and then the floor and handcuffed him. I then helped the woman try to stop the bleeding until the ambulance and other officers arrived. I held her breast closed with rubber gloves from my pocket. She was in shock and had lost a decent amount of blood. So much noise had been silenced so quickly. All that was left was her whimpering and my voice comforting. The radio crackled with sharp clips of other officers calling their arrival to dispatch with a

background of sirens. I was empty. I didn't have a thought, let alone an

emotion.

When I got home that night, I felt weary, not heroic or

courageous. I felt only a small, cold flame of hate that, like a pilot light,

stayed on. The boy inside my mind was suffering in quiet, but the Wolf

also was there—well fed and blazing in that tiny flame. I was supposed

to be at peace. I knew what I'd done was right, even brave. Yet I was

left with the afterbirth of what it had taken to manage the situation —

extreme fear, suppression, and violence. On the inside, I was scorched

to the point I felt charred under my skin. The feeling crushed all my

other emotions into that single tiny flame that held my hate for the

man who had done that to his wife, for the society that hadn't kept him

in jail, and for the God that allowed such pain to exist in the world. I

also felt the boy's hate for me, and that was soul crushing. Down deep,

in a place I dared not often look, I hated myself. I hated the hero I had

become.

When I got home I threw my uniform shirt into a biohazard

bag. It was stained with blood — mine and the douche bag's. My white

tee shirt had blood on it, too. I left it on because I was pretty sure it was my blood. My pants also were bloody but removing them would have required taking off my boots, which were too far down on my feet. It was about 7:45 in the morning. I grabbed a beer from the refrigerator and plopped on the couch, my legs resting on the coffee table. I had to spread around some beer cans with my feet to make room. Accidentally, I kicked some over. I guessed Randy, my roommate, had had a rough time in South Sector yesterday.

He came down to the living room in his uniform, ready for his day shift. He saw the blood, my beer, and the TV channel choice of Cartoon Network, and smiled.

"Rough night?" he asked.

"Yeah," I said. "Had to fight a crazy bastard who stabbed his wife and then tried to cut her nipple out. What about you?" Randy's smile remained but it was as empty as I knew mine was.

"Yeah," he said. "Suicide. Guy blew his head off with a shotgun and made a giant brain-wallpaper Jackson Pollock mess."

"Lovely," I said. "You get points for the Pollock reference, but we were looking for Kandinsky-Brain Splat for full credit." He sat down next to me, coffee in hand, and took a couple of sips as the Road

Runner managed to thwart the Coyote yet again. Then he stood up.

"Well, get some sleep," he said. "I'm going to go get me a Road

Runner, fuckface."

"Yeah, good luck," I said. "Throw me another beer on your way

out."

We were twenty-five then, washing out other people's blood

from our uniforms and washing back our tears with beer. The inner

dialogue already wouldn't stop. A voice from long ago said, *Don't hit*

and don't hate, little boy. It's not nice to hate. The wolf replied, *Shut the*

fuck up, little boy, stop crying. The wolf didn't feel my shame or pain

turn into the despair that came from not knowing what was right

anymore. My reality had changed from debating right and wrong to

going to work, being violent, and seeing violence. I was trying to stay

alive and keep others alive as my moral horizon shrank, collapsing the

ideals I'd held my whole life. There was no God on the street. There

was no Golden Rule, no Kantian Categorical Imperative, no Aristotelian

Ethics. There was just a steel wall behind which I was not capable of

judging the morality of any action that kept myself or others alive.

Deep down, though, I knew the truth: good people don't do bad things.

Chapter 11:

Close Your Eyes

Tight

"You're not a cop until you taste them."

—Rick Monticello of Somerdale Police

Department, New Jersey

December 1997, Nashville

Mike Goldman was a cop in the New York City Housing Authority Police Department before Mayor Rudolph Giuliani merged it and the transit police into the NYPD in 1995. He was bald with a mustache and a strong New York accent, which was even more pronounced among Nashville accents. He was my mentor and a great friend. When I met him, he also was going through a divorce, which, I was to learn, was almost common in Copland when a marriage hit the three- to five-year mark—the time it took for wives to realize their new husbands were cynical assholes who could barely function outside of Copland.

Now Copland isn't really a place; it's a state of mind. But it emerges slowly, and you don't realize you're in it until the voices in your life slowly grow silent because no one has anything to say to you, and you realize you don't have anything to say to them.

Mike was a fantastic police officer, one of the best I ever knew. He was a problem solver and dispute settler with excellent instincts and tactical intelligence. I tried to take as many calls with him as I could, especially during the first six months I was by myself. The two of us would walk up to a door in the projects, me standing on one side and Mike on the other. Mike would rap on the door with his baton or flashlight and yell, in the most out-of-place New York accent,

"Metropolitan Police Department, Officer Goldman. Open the door,

please!" Every time he yelled that, I busted a gut. No one ever expected

a German/Jewish cop from New York City to be at his or her door, and

it was hysterical. Mike would wait until we were right up to the door

and then say to me, "This call looks especially dangerous. You handle

it." It was his way of allowing me to learn how to take control of a

situation, calm tempers, and work out solutions, or quickly react to a

violent assault when a door opened. "Either way," Mike told me, "it

benefits both of us greatly."

I would handle the call until I was out of ideas or solutions or

running into tricky legal territory. Then I'd look over to Mike, who took

over handling the call while I switched to being the cover, or backup,

officer. I can't tell you how much I learned from Mike. He knew when

he could use humor and when he needed to quickly grab people before

they got really violent.

I learned one lesson I never forgot the night we were walking

through the projects to a 10-54P —subject with a gun. The women

who usually rented the public housing units and took care of all the

babies knew they could get a really quick police response by telling the dispatchers over the phone that their boyfriend, baby's daddy, or

whomever, was "beating on me and has a gun." So, oftentimes "guy

with gun" calls were fake. This call, which came in around midnight,

wasn't. As soon as we rounded the corner and looked at the address

numbered 541, the guy on its porch took off running, gun in hand.

Mike and I ran after the guy, headed toward what was called

The Creek. At these Preston Taylor projects were several buildings on

a long hill. Near the bottom were five or six more buildings built into a

horseshoe drive. We were running down the hill and were about one

hundred fifty yards from The Creek. As usual, the streetlights were

shot out because it's easier to deal dope in the dark. So it was really

dark. Chasing after someone is fun. Chasing after someone with a

partner is more fun. Chasing after someone at night in a dangerous

place is less fun. Chasing after someone with a gun at night in a

dangerous place is not fun. There is no real plan, just a lot of

threatening the guy as you run: "Drop that fucking gun!" or "Drop the

gun or we will shoot you!" You get bonus points for creativity and if

you can use a line from a movie. Anyway, you don't want to get too

close to the guy in case he turns and shoots you. For the same reason,

you can't tackle him, either.

When we reached The Creek, which was surrounded by brush
and trees, we stopped and shined our lights around the area. The
brush and trees surrounding The Creek disappeared after about
twenty yards, so there was no place the suspect could have run that
wasn't back toward open ground. If he'd done that, we would have
seen him come out. Behind The Creek was an open field with a really
shitty hill that no one likes to run up. Also, a bridge about thirty feet
long spanned The Creek, and you could run across it to the other side if
you were trying to make good time. It was a known rumor, however,
that cops would string high tensile-strength fishing line, impossible to
see at night, across the bridge. So no one ran across the bridge after
dark.

As we slowed down and scanned the creek and brush with our
lights, I tripped on a rock in the stream, fell hard, and smashed my
flashlight bulb on a rock. Not good. I was in a creek, in pitch-black
darkness, trying to find a guy who was hiding with a gun in his hand.
Mike handed me a little backup light he kept on his belt.

"Always keep two lights, fuckwad," Mike said. "I guess he got
away. We should go." I noticed he said that while shining his light in
the opposite direction he was looking. Following his gaze, I saw what

he saw — a piece of denim sticking out from a bush behind a rock.

What obligation did we have to risk our lives over this shitbag who had no doubt been locked up before and no doubt would be locked up ten more times in the next year for ten other things? Why not walk back to the apartment in safety and take a report? You could almost write the narrative without ever talking to anyone: Baby's daddy comes over and tries to get money or cook crack in the apartment or is pissed that baby's mama has a new man. Baby's mama gets mad. Daddy hits mama, threatens to shoot mama, and mama calls cops, *ad infinitum*. For me, there was a moral obligation to risk everything in the name of justice. Why? Because Daddy broke the law? Is law, then, the defining set of principles outlining our moral duty as humans? No, America itself was founded because we thought British law unjust and immoral. Instead, I felt a moral obligation to fight evil so that the good may thrive. I believed I was fighting God's fight. Doesn't the Bible even say that? It's right in Romans 13:4 (Douay-Rheims Bible 1899 American Edition): "For he is God's minister to thee, for good. But if thou do that which is evil, fear: for he beareth not the sword in vain. For he is God's minister: an avenger to execute wrath upon him that doth evil."

But Mike never agreed with me. When we discussed our obligation, I would say, "Blessed are the Peacemakers."

"It's just a job, fuckwad," he would reply.

So as we stood there in the dark, about to try to arrest a guy who could very well be one second away from killing one or both of us, I knew I was going to arrest him for the sake of fighting for good. Mike was going to arrest him because it was our job, and he wanted to do a good job. I was still a rookie, of course, and Mike had been a cop for eight years. Silently, we counted to three and hit the guy with our lights, our guns pointed and ready, physically and mentally, to pull those triggers. The douche didn't expect it. His gun was lying next to him. Unwilling to risk his draw to our trigger pull, he slowly turned over so we could handcuff him, as Mike kicked his gun away. Good triumphed that night, Mike did his job. The douche went to jail.

We cops constantly walk in the murky water of daily life, which often devastates our personal lives. Mike, for instance, had a daughter he desperately loved. The sad thing was that his wife had convinced him to leave New York for her new job in Nashville. Now that they had divorced, she was moving back up to New York with their daughter, and Mike had to stay in Nashville to work and pay child support. How bad does that suck?

A couple of years before I joined the Metro Police, Mike had been in a gunfight. The suspect shooting at him had been hiding behind a car and Mike had ingeniously thought to skip his bullets off the asphalt underneath the vehicle. I always wondered if I would have thought of that, or died that day. Point is, I think that's the day that, for Mike, the job became "just a job." But maybe that's just my own transference of how I felt after my shooting. Or maybe I'm just plain wrong. I think Mike wanted the job to be more, but the so-called ends simply became everything for him while the means used to achieve those ends became irrelevant.

Conversely, I thought that if being a police officer meant you risked your family life, death, and soul to darkness, it had to be more than just a job. We were special because we were fighting an epic battle of good and evil, of the just battling the unjust. We had to win. If we didn't, society would fall. I didn't believe I was on a jihad or that my job was a fatwa giving me God's authority to dispense justice as I saw fit. I simply believed I was doing good. Between Mike and me, the issue was never resolved. We agreed to disagree, and life went on.

One day we were doing a walk-through. We walked through the projects and turned corners to see who was holding a gun, who ran, or who was selling crack or powder. Someone always ran. Anyway, we heard screaming near the horseshoe and saw a woman yelling and pointing at the bushes even as she backed away. We ran over and looked at the ground. In a brown bush, a plant really, was a dead baby girl with a little pink bow in her hair. She obviously had fallen from the window above the front door. A breeze gently moved a small white blanket, back and forth, as it hung, almost tenderly, from the window. Mike gently picked up the girl's body and I knew he was picturing his own little girl. I knew he was thinking how little her life must have meant to someone, and I knew the thought was impossible for him to grasp. Sadness turned to incredulity, then to outrage, as Mike and I attempted to piece together what had happened. We searched the house, suspecting a possible double murder or murder/suicide. But no one had been inside.

The lady who found the poor child had answers, though, and she was shouting them to the heavens and anyone who would listen. The mother was Lashonda, a crackhead who often left her kids to get crack, which meant offering herself to the dealer. Whenever that happened, she was gone for a while, leaving her kids to stay home alone. Yes, she had another child, who, thank God, was running around the neighborhood and not home. We found out who her dealer was. While on our way to his place to arrest her, we found her walking back to her apartment. I remember that she was too high to even cry when we took her to jail, but that's all I remember.

A week later, Mike and I were dispatched to an apartment near West End Avenue near Vanderbilt University, a nice area downtown. Dispatch informed us that the caller had stated her husband wasn't answering the phone and that she was worried because he'd been talking weirdly all day. The caller had gone to pick up their daughter and wanted us to check on him. She wouldn't be home for about twenty minutes. We drove to the address and knocked on the door. Mike did his usual routine.: "You take this call," he said. "It seems dangerous." Even after we knocked and called out several times, no one came to the door. Not uncommon.

We walked around the apartment and looked in windows. I had to jump to peer into the bathroom window on the ground floor, and I saw what you hope you don't see. A man was lying in a bathtub filled with red water — so red, it looked maroon. I told Mike. We went back to the front door, smashed it open, and searched the house,

finishing in the bathroom. The man had dark hair, was naked, and

clearly had committed suicide. We called for an ambulance, Criminal

Investigation Department, Homicide, and a supervisor, per SOP.

Unfortunately, though, we didn't make it back to the front door before

the wife and daughter burst into the bedroom and saw past us to their

husband and father, respectively. The wife screamed. Mike grabbed

the girl who was, I would guess, about seven years old, just about the

same age as his daughter, Samantha. He picked her up and carried her

quickly out of the bedroom and downstairs, asking her what her

favorite color is and if she liked to sing songs and telling her Mommy

was upset about something but would be right back down. I grabbed

the woman as she tried to run into the bathroom. She fell, limp, into

my arms and sobbed so loudly, I thought she would burst. I thought I

might, too.

"You're not a cop until you've tasted them" – tasted your tears

mixed with those of strangers.

It took me a long time to figure out why Mike would keep

telling me, "It's only a job." He kept a picture of his daughter on the

dash of his police car, taped near the mileage reader. He said he wanted her with him always, no matter how many miles he drove

without her there. He had lost the woman he loved more than any

other woman in the world as well as the little girl he loved more than

life. His wife and daughter had been his reasons for being. So when he

drove around the projects, responding to danger after danger, he was

just doing a job. He'd lost everything that mattered in his life. So what

if he died?

That's the lesson I'd learned from the incident with Larry

Charles in the parking lot of the Circle K: maybe our moral obligation

to achieve certain ends mattered more than the means we used. I was

slowly learning that I was losing my soul, realizing that pieces of me

were being destroyed. If I was becoming ruined, this had to be more

than a job, right? Maybe the battle was epic because it wasn't about

good and evil. Maybe it was about finding a way to save my own soul.

What should a cop love more than his or her own soul? How much is

thirty pieces of silver worth? What do you get for the silver? What is

this "value" I must die for? I can see killing the bad so the good shall

live. But I don't understand fighting in an arena where a tiger is

released for every lion killed, and a lion is born for every tiger

defeated.

Chapter 12:

Down the Rabbit

Hole

"I can't go back to yesterday because I was a different person then."

— Lewis Carroll, *Alice in Wonderland*

January 1998, Nashville

The Greeks debated the question of whether an object which

has had all its components replaced remains fundamentally the same

object. The paradox is most notably recorded by Plutarch in *Life of*

Theseus from the late first century. Plutarch asked whether a ship

which was restored by replacing each and every one of its wooden

parts, remained the same ship. Let us say, for example, that a ship

called the Queen Mary is leaving the Port of New York and New Jersey

and is scheduled to arrive in Miami in a week's time. The Queen Mary

is carrying a payload of wooden planks. Along the way, one of her old

planks springs a leak and is replaced with one of the new planks from

the payload.

Shortly thereafter, several more leaks occur and, eventually,

each of the old wooden planks is replaced with a new one from the

payload. When the Queen Mary arrives in Miami, all of the new planks

from the original payload have been used to repair the ship, which is

now carrying a payload of the old, wooden planks. Now, which is the

Queen Mary—the ship that left New York or the ship that arrived in

Miami? After only eighteen months in Copland, many of my wooden

planks — the planks that made up the core of my belief system and the

foundation of who I believed I was as a moral person — already had

been replaced by new, cold, steel planks. I was changing. I was changed.

Now you've caught up with me in January 1998, the month of the bank robber and the Suntrust Bank. "He's behind Hunan Express in a white Bonneville," the radio squawked. Of course, he wasn't "in the Bonneville." He was hiding behind it. Did I mention I kicked away his guns from near his hands as he lay dying, bleeding, dead – whatever he was in those seconds? I had the distinct feeling that I knew to do that from the movies, though I couldn't remember which one— the cop or detective— was supposed to kick away the guns. Maybe all of them did. Regardless, the trauma of a police shooting is well documented because it's usually a zero to kill-or-be-killed moment that's over in seconds. In the United States, two-thirds of officers suffer from some distress, moderate or severe, after they're involved in a shooting incident, according to the American Academy of Experts in Traumatic Stress. A total of 70 percent leave the force within seven years. The department gave me three days off, calling them "Traumatic Incident Days." That's all they really knew to do back then, I guess.

The following Monday, I had to talk to the department psychologist and get cleared to go back to work. Everyone knew to never say anything to two people in the world, no matter what —the

psychologist and the representative from the internal affairs

department. Terry Delance, my friend who'd just gone through the

"After Shooting Shrink" process —or ASS, as we called it —a year

earlier, picked me up and drove me. At the psychologist's office, I

smiled and talked about how I wasn't having nightmares or suicidal

thoughts, how I still felt safe, and other horseshit. I was cleared and

went back to work Tuesday. But I began to rot inside. I just couldn't

quite feel it yet.

I can't tell you how scared I was on Tuesday, my first day back.

I'd barely slept. My first serious call Tuesday came one hour into the

shift. It was a standard "Project Domestic," as we called them. A

woman called the police and said her "baby's daddy" was there with a

gun. These calls went out all day, every day. In her defense, he

probably was just there and he probably did have a gun. But all the

knuckleheads would leave before we got there. I was dispatched to the

call. So was Officer Mike Martin. When I pulled into the projects, my

blood was slamming through my arteries. As adrenaline coursed

through me, my hands and arms grew cold. I turned my car onto the

horseshoe dead end and parked. Deathly frightened, I struggled to breathe. My head pounded. I knew I was going to be shot. I knew it. I

exited my car and walked toward the address, my head pivoting as I

looked for the direction from which certain death would come. I was

almost limping to the address, trying to keep a tree, a car, anything, in

front of me, as cover, in the event shooting started.

Mikey pulled into the horseshoe drive, too, and exited his

vehicle. I waited for him, certain that every second I stood there in the

open was the last second of my life. I'd been on this type of call one

hundred times. For Mikey, it must have been a thousand times. Almost

always, they turned into a report. They were a typical way for a fed-up

woman to get rid of her drug-dealing, gun-toting baby's daddy when

he acted up: She'd call the police. He'd leave. We'd show up and take a

report. Usually, that would quiet things down for the rest of the day.

Occasionally, we'd see the guy coming from the apartment and

would have to chase him down and fight him. Domestics were always

dangerous, but my point is, this was a very routine domestic in the

projects, and I was almost frozen in fear. To this day, I am utterly

ashamed that I took up a position slightly behind Mikey as we walked.

One hand on my gun, I was ready at any moment to defend the two of

us. My brain was in overdrive. When the woman burst from her apartment, I was certain the shooting would start. But no, she was alone—angry, but alone. Her baby's daddy had fled through the back door several minutes earlier, she said, and likely was headed toward the playground area. She was uninjured and had not been assaulted, so she changed her story from "had a gun" to "might have had a gun, I don't really remember now." We took the report and left.

As we were standing outside, Mikey packed a nice dip of Skoal Classic and asked me, "How are you doing?"

"I'm fine, doing fine," I said. "OK, I guess."

"Well, that's good," he replied. "I don't know how you're supposed to feel. I've never shot nobody. But I can't imagine you feel fine. Let me know if you need anything."

Then, as if on cue—you couldn't make it up—a call came over the radio: "Attention all cars. All cars, 1054-PE, 16th and Charlotte, Caller advised at the U-Haul parking lot one male chasing another with a gun." Mikey and I were at 17th and Charlotte. I saw the U-Haul across the street, and I had a decision point: *What cop was I going to be? Who was I on the inside?* I could have gotten into my car and followed Mikey to the U-Haul and played it safe. Mikey was twenty years older and he was going to drive there, as well he should. But I knew I could sprint

the distance and be there in fifteen seconds. I could engage the armed

guy myself and cut him off before he got to the street where I was

standing and escaped into the projects. Fear was flowing through me. I

was still certain I was going to die every second. So I ran with the fear.

I ran with all I had toward that U-Haul, maybe to commit suicide,

maybe to overcome the fear, once and for all. As I crossed the street

and stepped onto the parking lot, I saw that the suspect, jogging

toward the back of the store, had a silver handgun.

"Police!" I yelled, with a ferocity that would have stopped a

tiger. At full speed, I continued, drawing my gun (I'd learned

something) and pointing it at the suspect. "Drop the gun or I kill you,

motherfucker!" I wasn't rational. I wasn't me. I wanted to kill him. He

was my pain. I was going to kill my pain.

The suspect threw the gun under a parked brown station

wagon and kept running, but he was done. I holstered my gun and

sprinted. As he turned the corner around the back of the U-Haul, I

slammed into him. His head hit the pavement as I cushioned my fall

with his skull. I hit him twice with my elbow in the face. I spun him

onto his stomach and handcuffed him. There was nothing in his pockets but a crack rock. I retrieved the gun under the car. Walking back toward him, I pointed his own gun at him and yelled, "Will this fire, motherfucker! What happens if I pull the fucking trigger, motherfucker!?" I was rage, embodied—not a man, not a cop, just an emotion. Mikey took the gun out of my hand.

"What the fuck are you doing?" he said. "Give me that. I'll take him to booking, man. You just go get some coffee or take your dinner." Mikey tossed me a pair of his handcuffs and put the suspect in his car. When he came back to me, he saw me shaking with adrenaline and anger.

"Look, Ry," he said, "I don't know what you're going through, but you got to calm down. You're going to get yourself killed doing that shit."

Yeah, he was right. But the fear was gone. I had won. I was going to be OK. Behold the twin conquerors of fear—hate and rage.

Chapter 13:

Get Into Character

or Die

"Kathy, I'm lost," I said, though I knew she was sleeping.

"I'm empty and aching and I don't know why."

—Paul Simon, "America"

Spring 1998, Nashville

In February 1998, after I shot the bank robber, I was selected to work undercover in the Crime Suppression Unit of the Vice Division,

which handled street-level drugs and prostitution in Nashville. The

economic boom of the 1990s, the massive increase in Crack Indices

from 1984 to 2000, and the orchestration of so many drugs and guns

by the various large gangs—Crips, Bloods, Gangster Disciples, MS-13—

made the 1990s a rough time for undercover narcotics officers.

Tennessee has the dubious distinction of having one of the

worst violent crime rates in the country. According to the FBI Uniform

Crime Report, as of this writing, the state ranks fourth, with an

estimated 579.7 violent crimes for every 100,000 residents. I'm just

trying to put my rich-kid-from-Kansas background in perspective

when I talk about running around undercover in an environment

where all the drug dealers were armed. Anyone who has done any

dangerous undercover work has been changed by it. For me, the

change was instantaneous, at least internally. Externally, I grew a

goatee and let my hair grow longer than the short crew cut that so

identifies anyone in the police or military. Guys who work narcotics

always will tip their caps to other guys in narcotics because the job is

indescribable with respect to fear, danger, and pure vulnerability.

Their families each will tell you the same story about how their brother, husband, son, daughter, or sister has been changed. Their

families will tell you the happy part of their loved ones is gone. They

will talk about how the vulnerability necessary to work the job forced

their family member, in off-hours, to create an impenetrable wall.

What do walls do? They keep things in and they keep things out.

Family members know they're shut out. They will lower their heads

when they tell you how their loved one used to be. Then they will tell

you how they hope he retires soon. But you can never go home again.

Those walls will never go down, no matter how long or short a time a

cop worked the beat.

A police officer in uniform is instantly recognizable and carries

a certain gravitas in society. When the uniform comes off, it definitely

feels as if a part of you has come off, too. Being in plain clothes changes

the ground rules in a lot of ways, including how people react to you.

For instance, when you first see a cop in your rearview mirror, your

stomach jumps a little and you glance at your speed. Instantly, you

check if you're doing anything wrong. If a cop walks up to you or rings

your doorbell, you instantly feel a little bit of panic and think: *Is*

everything OK? What did I do? Is my spouse or child OK? What did that

little bastard do? How about when you're lost and see a cop on the corner. Instantly, you feel safe, knowing that, most of the time, the cop

will make an honest attempt to help you.

Put on a hoodie, torn jeans, and work boots, and hide your

badge and gun, and it all changes. Cars don't see your undercover car

and slow down. People don't see your uniform and act accordingly.

Since the undercover cop spends most of his or her time in the worst

parts of cities, there are a great many other predators around.

Interestingly, some drug dealers can see undercover cops a mile away.

They recognize another predator on the prowl.

I was working around legends at the Metro Nashville Police

Department. I thought they were legends, anyway, and I aspired to be

just as tough as they were. The guys on this unit had iron in them and

felt nothing. They did their jobs while story after story was told about

them. The Crime Suppression Unit numbered one lieutenant, two

sergeants, and ten to twelve undercover detectives. Part of the job was

buying drugs on the street, sometimes posing as a dealer, other times

as a buyer. Part of the job was executing high-risk search warrants on

drug-related properties. In Nashville, in the mid-'80s, Metro Police

formed an anti-gang task force to investigate whether some of the

crime in Nashville was related to gangs. By the end of that decade, they'd identified ten to fifteen gangs in Davidson County. During the

'90s, Jamal Shakir, leader of the Rollin' 90s Crips gang, arrived from

Los Angeles. From 1994 to 1997, Shakir operated a multi–state drug

and money laundering business from a house in East Nashville. He also

orchestrated the murders of nine people across the country.

At the same time, Shakir was setting up shop, the economic

boom of the 1990s brought other gangs to Middle Tennessee. When

the state enacted TennCare, free health insurance for the poor, it

attracted even more low- income and troubled families. By the time

TennCare almost bankrupted Tennessee, the damage was done in

terms of crime. Families from large cities, such as Atlanta, Detroit,

Chicago and Los Angeles, already had moved to Tennessee for the free

health insurance. Some brought along their troubled youth.

Homegrown gangs emerged. A federal grand jury did not indict Shakir

until 1999. Ultimately, he was convicted of orchestrating multiple

murders and distributing cocaine, crack, and marijuana, and received

sixteen sentences of life without parole. Yet he was only one individual

in a city that grew increasingly violent. The two units set up to combat

the violence were Crime Suppression Unit (CSU), the street-level drug

unit, and FLEX, the latter to target high-crime and homicide areas. I spent three years on one or the other. CSU was the first.

On CSU, we'd pull up to people in our cars and try to buy crack. We'd walk around the alleys and parking lots behind motels. We were wherever we could buy crack from the most dangerous dealers. One of the most effective ways to close down a dope house was to find a crackhead to be a source. Specific laws exist to verify for the courts the veracity of an official Confidential Informant (CI) before his or her testimony is admissible and before it can be used to obtain a search warrant or other legal documents. But using such a CI sometimes took time and multiple drug buys. My CSU also could have been known as the "Let's Get Everyone and Let God Sort Them Out" unit. We'd see a crackhead walking in a crime-ridden area, stop him, and pay him to get drugs for us.

If the crackhead outright stole the twenty dollars, you can guess what would happen. Or maybe you can't because you aren't that violent. We'd find him where he'd bought the crack and was trying to smoke it, usually some close-by place. We'd jump out and beat the ever-living shit out of him. We'd explain that stealing was wrong, and then give him a chance to fix his mistake by going back to the house. You see, the world of violence is run by fear. If you dare to enter it and then dare to try to control it, you must do so through fear. The biggest

shark with the sharpest teeth controls the other fish. If you aren't as

scary as the biggest, scariest shark, you don't matter.

If the crackhead brought the crack back to us, though, we'd

identify ourselves as police and ask him where he got it. Of course we

usually had people watching where he went, but often it was

impossible to really tell without exposing our surveillance. If he was

willing to buy his freedom for that night with information, which he or

she usually was, we'd get him to go back and try to buy more with one

of us. Our goal was to observe crack in the house in plain view. With a

little stretch of the plain view and hot pursuit doctrines, we could

legally enter the house or apartment. So imagine a crackhead and

undercover standing at the porch trying to buy more crack or heroin

or whatever: Thugs go back to the kitchen or living room table, upon

which there usually were drugs and several guns, to retrieve more of

the drug. The undercover cop "accidentally" wonders inside or gets

enough of a glance to ascertain that drugs and guns are in the house.

The undercover and crackhead purchase drugs, turn and leave, but,

just as they do, the rest of us, dressed in raid gear and jeans, storm

through the doors and windows, and use as much force as necessary to affect the arrest. Inside the house, the dope dealers fight, knock down,

punch, run, jump, escape tackles, and try to shoot and dodge our

takedown team.

Once we had everyone in handcuffs, we'd classify all the

evidence and suspects, and then either do it again down the street, all

night long, or sell the dope from the house as if we were the dope

dealers. Plan A yielded good results and caught big fish. Plan B, which

usually was much less dangerous, also was quite hilarious. This was

back before cell phones were common and most people used pagers

and public phones. Basically, the dope dealer's pager would go off and

we'd wait for the buyer to come to the door. When people arrived and

tried to buy at the front door, we'd yank them inside.

The most common job of CSU was "buy busts," which was a

new idea in the early and mid-'90s. Basically, one or two guys drive

around and buy drugs from drug dealers who stand in alleyways, on

cul-de-sacs, and outside apartments and public project housing. Then,

the rest of us jump out and try to arrest them. This can go smoothly or

can cause literal pandemonium. Usually, it results in a foot chase and

quite the fight for whoever makes the initial tackle until others catch

up and help exact retribution. The first day I was on CSU, I was given my new partner, who became one of my favorite people in the world.

Edward Kessel had gone to Vanderbilt and played linebacker for the

San Francisco 49ers for a short time. It's too bad Hollywood never

picked him up. He would have made wrestler-turned-actor Dwayne

"The Rock" Johnson cringe in fear. Kessel, who had a deep voice, was a

huge black guy that looked like he had played linebacker, but was

probably, we all joked, too mean to be in the NFL. He loved his fellow

cops with all his heart, though, and he was my favorite. The first night

we worked together, we were in his car and he had a big chew in his

mouth as he explained the ropes. It was clear he always called dealers

"motherfuckers."

"Now look, son, here is not 'wearing a uniform policing,'" he

said. "You don't have no uniform, so they won't play your games. They

may not try to kill you as much in your uniform because they know

they can probably skip whatever charges you are going to lay on them.

But these motherfuckers will try to kill you out here undercover

because they know they are FUCKED if you catch them.

"They know a Uniform sees them, they may or may not chase

them, may or may not catch them," he went on. "They never get close

enough to be able to testify to what they saw in court. Uniforms can get them on 'possession of drug' or 'selling drug' but the selling will get

reduced because it's just based on the amount. And rarely are those

motherfuckers stupid enough to let a uniform in a Marked actually see

them sell the dope. Plus, they know most uniform cars are just there to

answer calls and to make sure no one is blatantly shooting anybody

when they drive by.

"They see us come, son, it is ON," he added. "They know they

just sold to US. Hear? They know they are going to get prison for the

gun they are carrying and the selling or distribution charge we are

going to lay on their motherfucking asses."

"I got you, Kessel," I said, toughly as I could. Being white and

five foot eight, I just wasn't pulling it off like Kessel's six-foot-two

linebacker frame. But I was trying.

"You better get me, son, because let me explain this to you

again: There are NO Rules, got that? None," he said. "You think there

are rules out here, now, in these jeans, you will be a dead cop.

Understand now?"

"I gotcha," I said. We'd been driving around and our

undercover officer had just bought from a guy who was quickly walking away — toward us. The radio crackled from the Undercover's hidden mic: "Deal's done, deal's done, male black, black sweatshirt, jeans, headed north on East 6th, toward you, Kessel."

"I got 'em'," Kessel said into the radio. He turned toward me. "All right, son, I'm going to put him right on you." This was all happening way too fast. I didn't know what he meant. At the last second, he swerved the car and put my passenger side "right on" the suspect. I jumped out, face to face, with the suspect and yelled, "Police!" Now, if you could have freeze framed that moment, you would have seen Kessel proceed to shake his head and say, "Son, didn't I just say that there are 'no rules' and that these motherfuckers know they are going down in a bad way if we catch them? Didn't I just tell you all that? Then what the fuck are you shouting 'Police!' for?" That's what he would have said.

The thug reared back and punched me in the face, knocking me over, right before he went to sprint away. Instead, he was hit by a six-foot-two former linebacker for the '49s. I heard the breath leave his lungs as he was slammed onto the sidewalk. Blood ran down my face. I looked up to see Kessel return the favor as the thug's nose exploded. Kessel was lecturing the thug on what happens when you hit a cop in the face. It was not a nice lecture at all and Kessel was being —

demonstrative. I had picked myself up by then and, while someone

took the thug to the ambulance he now needed, I was about to get a

lecture as well from Kessel. Mine was short.

"Understand now, stupid motherfucker?" he asked.

"Yes."

"You OK? Need to go to the hospital?"

"No, I'm fine," I said. I was bleeding above the nose and was

going to have a nice black eye, but my pride was in way more pain at

that moment.

"Good. This motherfucker won't hit another officer for a while

now," Kessel said. "He will think real hard about it the next time.

Maybe save your dumbass from getting punched again. Now get back

in the car. UC (Undercover) is over on 8th now."

I learned the rule quickly: there are no rules. There weren't.

There were some cases that got convictions, and some cases that

didn't. But there, in the middle of the night, there couldn't be any rules

for us because there were no rules for them. Once, my night was dedicated to purchasing drugs at a single large motel on a lovely gang-

lined street near a public housing project we called Settle Court.

Dressed shabbily and smelling of urine and booze — my crackhead

uniform — I was invited into one of the motel rooms to purchase crack

cocaine. I was wired at the time, had a small revolver hidden in my

pants, and was carefully watched by undercover officers who were

scattered relatively close by. Unfortunately, as I was led into the room,

two guys knocked me to the ground, and a silver semiautomatic

revolver was pressed into my mouth. It was a shitty hotel room in the

shittiest part of town. My mind screamed. It screamed and screamed.

As I waited, paralyzed, I stared into the face of a monster and the

monster stared back. The world of color disappeared and tightened

into the darkened view of the gun and the face of the monster. I stared,

as if looking at Medusa, and actually felt a large part of my soul turning

to stone. I wasn't just staring at a piece-of-shit dope dealer with

nothing to lose, thinking he ruled the world because he ruled my life. I

was watching the last remnants of who I wanted to be blacken and

turn to ash. I felt emotions shutting off and parts of my mind sparking

out. The wolf inside me howled with power, knowing he had taken

over my soul and that the boy from Kansas was at long last dying.

When I was able to refocus several seconds later, I had lost a

tremendous part of me that cared about anything except survival. I
don't mean survival from just the situation at hand. I mean survival
from the pain inside — survival from the blackness that was
suffocating my mind and soul. I was devolving into two parts: the
violent wolf and the ever diminishing boy who just wanted the pain to
stop.

There was nothing in that room of value. There was nothing I
was doing there that was worth my life. I wasn't a hero. I was dressed
as a crackhead in the shittiest place I could imagine trying to spend
fifty bucks to buy drugs I didn't even use. I was playing dress-up in a
high-stakes game for my life. No one could see me. I was not moving
mountains. I was not even changing lives. I was bait to lure fish we
would catch, fish who were killing themselves over the crack. There
was no glory there. But there was — to us. We were fighting a war no
one truly knew about. We were in combat situations daily. We were at
war in the projects and the ghettos and the only emotion ever lapped
on us was hate. I knew then that I would never leave my brothers and
that I could not ever leave law enforcement knowing that this war was
going on. I would die here with them. I would stay here and die with
them, and I accepted that fact, and that fact made me very, very strong.

After a couple of minutes, the thug was done demonstrating his power and he stood me up, turned me around, and pushed me toward the door, away from the other two guys. As soon as the gun was removed from my mouth, I said my rehearsed sentence, "Ain't this bad in Detroit or Texas!"

"Shut the fuck up and walk!" the guy said, pushing me out the motel door with the gun in my back. But I had given the two code words — "Detroit" meaning "Suspect is armed with a gun" and "Texas" meaning "Officer in Serious Danger." I hoped everyone knew where I was and how badly I needed them.

"Where are we going?" I pleaded. "Just let me buy some rock, man. Let me go."

"Keep walking," the thug said. "It's down the stairs."

"Where down the stairs, down the concrete stairs?" I asked. "Man, I bought it at the Hojo motel last time, not behind it!" I was desperately trying to let the close cover officers know where I was, give them some location to find me. The thug pushed the gun into my back.

"Walk, motherfucker," he said, "down the stairs." We walked,
me calculating when to make my last stand and scan desperately for
my guys. As we got down the stairs, he pushed me toward a broken-
down single-wide trailer about one hundred feet behind the motel. My
heart was no longer racing, no longer panicked. I was ruined stone
now. I was unable to be affected. I planned to drop to the ground, get
the revolver from my crotch, roll to my right, and unload all five
rounds into the suspect. I was pretty sure only one of us was going to
make it to the trailer, and I knew that one was going to be me, or
neither of us. As I scanned the area, we left the safety of the motel's
concrete walkway and second-floor overhang and headed toward the
trailer. We were twenty feet away when I saw my guys and almost
laughed out loud. I cannot describe what true salvation feels like. I
know ministers and priests talk about it in church all the time. I know
religious scholars have studied it through the centuries. I know it's the
goal of every Christian. But I know what it feels like. It feels like all the
lights in your soul were dark and then someone threw a switch, and
they all came back on, at the same time. I looked at salvation. It was all
around me — seven of my brothers wearing black balaclava masks.
Two stood at the trailer with MP5 submachine guns pointed at us.
They flipped the switch with their thumbs, clicking on the red laser

site, aligning both red dots onto the suspect's face. When the shitbag

behind me looked at their laser sites align on him, he failed to see the

brutal attack coming from both sides and behind as two of my guys

appeared from the side of the motel and a third stepped out from

behind the lone tree we'd just passed. I dove to the left, out of the way,

just in time to see the suspect drop, unconscious, behind me.

In the meantime, the rest of the CSU team kicked open the door

to the room where I'd been held. I walked slowly back toward the

motel, knowing it was only 10 p.m. and I had four more hours left of

buying dope. I ducked behind a corner of the motel and threw up. No

one saw me. I had learned the lesson again: there are no rules.

After about a year, I was transferred off CSU and onto the West

FLEX unit. Some politics going on at the captain level punished my

sergeant and his guys. But I found adventure elsewhere, rest assured.

In one way, I wished I could have stayed in Narcotics on that CSU team.

In another way, I knew what that job was doing to me. Still, given the

choice, I think that kind of suicide might have been an OK one. I

returned to the uniformed division with remarkable knowledge of

where crime occurred and who was really doing what. I knew what

was happening behind the scenes after the marked police cars drove away. Our FLEX unit worked a lot with CSU and did some undercover

work of our own. It was full of great guys and we became very close as

we continued getting shot at, assaulted, and ran from—all part of our

daily adventures in the projects.

Chapter 14:

Upon the Rack

It requires more courage to suffer than to die.

— Napoleon Bonaparte

March 2000, Nashville

The same lack of self-preservation that pushes a cop toward —
not away from — the aimed gun keeps him from taking care of himself
or letting others help him after he is hurt. Oftentimes the hurt can't be
seen on the outside, save for a furtive wipe of the eyes, a quiet sigh, or
the sound of a swallow. We all hurt on the inside, where the pain is far

worse. Courage often is analyzed not by the men in the arena, but rather by the critic who, in the words of Teddy Roosevelt, "points out how the strong man stumbles, or where the doer of deeds could have done them better."

People who battle cancer are courageous. When they win, we cheer their victory. When they lose, we are saddened but still admire their bravery and effort. Other people are courageous with moral decisions, taking action in the face of threats to their person, reputation, position, job, status, and other hard-earned achievements. We admire whistleblowers and crime victims who come forth to prosecute or testify against their aggressor. Then there are those we may never know but who nevertheless refuse to comply with the unjust actions of those around them. But for the police officer, courage quite often is attached to sadness. I've learned that courage for the cop often results in paradoxical feelings. Courage in the face of danger doesn't necessarily mean anything good happened in the end.

Once, a thug —let's call him Dwayne—decided to try to kill a Nashville cop. The intelligence got back to us in two ways. First, Dwayne's girlfriend told the intelligence division after she was arrested for drugs. Second, Dwayne kept trying to kill one of us cops. I don't recall exactly what every single arrest warrant affidavit said; I

do, however, recall that he had ten warrants against him — almost all

by cops, three of them for attempted homicide. He'd tried to ram an

officer on a traffic stop with a stolen Cadillac in the Settle Court

projects, and then fled. He'd tried to shoot two officers trying to arrest

him for drugs, and then fled. He'd beaten his "baby's mother"

unconscious and left his baby to die in the trash can of her apartment,

and then fled. As you can imagine, a great deal of spare time was spent

on Dwayne's hideouts, the latest car he'd stolen, and how we could

catch him before he killed a cop or anyone else. Unfortunately, a great

deal of time also had been spent on unsuccessfully chasing Dwayne.

The latest intelligence was that he had "borrowed" a Cadillac

from the grandmother of his new girlfriend (the one who'd been

arrested) and was somewhere in West Sector. I was assigned to West

FLEX. Of course, we'd driven around our projects and looked at crack

houses, ghetto hot spots, alleyways, hiding spots, and every other nook

and cranny in which we thought the car might be stashed. For a week,

we'd had much as luck as everyone else, which is to say none. Felicia

Street was a small side street that ran between 26th Avenue North and

28th Avenue North and, for the span of those two small blocks, parallel to the major Charlotte Avenue. Felicia Street is bulldozed into

nothingness now, but it was a line of crack houses and broken-down

apartments for street whores, crackheads, squatters, and anyone else

of top breeding. But there was this one house on the corner of 26th

North and Felicia Street, with its back to Charlotte Avenue, its front to

Felicia Street, that was just a little bit nicer than the others. And lo,

verily I say unto thee, guess what we saw in the driveway there one

sunny afternoon? The Cadillac. It hadn't been there an hour earlier.

Then, there it was. Now, this didn't mean Dwayne was there. It just

meant the Cadillac was there. But it did mean we probably could get a

search warrant for the house. It also meant that whoever was inside

that house wasn't leaving, no matter what.

My partner, Greg, and I called the FLEX unit. Six of us

surrounded the house. Three of us—me, Greg, and Sgt. Briton—

approached the front door, guns out but kept low. Greg had his tactical

shotgun ready as Sgt. Briton knocked hard on the door. After several

minutes, the girlfriend came to the door, completely unfazed by seeing

three armed cops, multiple police cars in front of her house, and

several more cops surrounding the place. She opened the door.

"What the fuck do you want?" she asked.

"Look here, Miss, you know why we're here," Sgt. Briton said. "Now stop the bullshit. He in here?"

"Maybe he is," she said. "Maybe he isn't."

"Look here, Miss, we are getting a search warrant for your place right now," Sgt. Briton said. "If you tell us he's not here and we go in there and find him, you are going to jail for another felony for harboring a fugitive. If he's in there and he kills someone, you are going to jail for accessory to murdering a police officer. You understand that? We will make sure you go to the chair with your boyfriend. Now I'm going to ask you this once, straight up: Is Dwayne in there?" She stepped onto the porch and slammed the door.

"Yeah, he's in there," she said. "He's got a shotgun too and he's going to kill the first cop that walks in that house. So fuck you. I'm done." She was taken to one of the cars and held as we waited for the search warrant. Sgt. Briton Greg and I had retreated from the house. We all discussed our options.

When the search warrant arrived, we had "the stack" ready to go. The stack is that line of cops or soldiers you see busting into houses and buildings. The line is set up in a particular order on the basis of gun selections, layout of the house/structure, how entry is going to be made, who is going to ram the door, and more. Members of a stack each have a particular responsibility based on their positions in the line and what happens in front of them. The first person through the door, for instance, may have the responsibility of dealing with the first threat in the first room, unless they can push forward to the farthest point of the house, perhaps down a long hallway. If the first man or woman in a stack peels off to address a threat, the second one pushes onward toward the farthest point. Guys armed only with their semiautomatic Glocks are spaced throughout the stack and are able to holster quickly and fight or handcuff suspects, while guys with MP5s or shotguns continue to push through the layout of the house or dwelling, making sure no more armed threats exist.

We'd also spoken about the reality of the threat: there was a good chance this was going to end with some blood spilled. Have you ever played hide and seek? Have you ever played hide and seek in the dark with flashlights? Now close your eyes. Imagine playing hide and seek in the dark with flashlights inside a house that's wholly new to you. In fact, you don't even know its layout. Oh, and you're "it." If the person you're playing against can jump out and see you before you see them, you die. Not so fun a game now. So, the first guy in the stack, the guy who enters first, is the crazy guy. I always wanted to be that guy but also never wanted to be that guy. The raw fear and adrenaline that explodes through you when the door bursts open and you enter is amazing and addictive. However, the intellectual part of your brain analyzes what you're doing, sounds alarms, and tries to shout louder than your inner wolf, who wants nothing more than to kill. The intellectual part of the brain has run the numbers and, rightly, concluded that entering this house, in any order, is a bad idea for the continuance of your existence. To accentuate the point in this instance, the intellectual part of my brain released every chemical possible to make me throw up. But, alas, the wolf ruled. The wolf wanted to go first, and he did.

There was no need for a violent entry filled with flash bang grenades, shattered windows, and shouts of "Police! Police! Drop your weapons!" This one began with the door pushed open slowly and quietly, and the silence of flashlight beams from the end of gun barrels sweeping throughout the doorway first, trying to illuminate as much as possible of the kill zone. In silence, I led the stack into the front room. There was a tan chair in the front room—turned over and pulled against the corner of the wall, as a makeshift barrier, so someone could

hide behind it. My stomach and brain were frozen. It was all I could do

to turn my gaze away from the chair, from the place where my death

could come in seconds. My job as first in the stack was to pass the large

first room and continue pushing onward toward the farthest point of

the house—the back bedrooms. In every movie where an armed

executioner pulls out his gun and tells the victim to "start walking, "

the victim just can't bring himself to turn his back to his executioner.

He or she pleads and walks backward, unable to fully turn and feel

death strike from behind. I felt that terror as I went past the chair

toward the back bedrooms, waiting a full second while my brain

screamed in panic. Then there was more of the same silence as

noiseless light scanned nooks and corners, the only sound our

shuffling feet, breathing, and the soft jingling of metal against metal.

No one was behind the chair.

     I continued pushing forward and turned right at the end of the

hall into one of the bedrooms. Straight in front of me was the bed,

headboard pushed against the wall on the left side of the room and a

window, closed, looking back at me from the other side of the room. I

slammed myself back against the wall as I saw the sliding closet door ajar. The closet was on the same side of the room as the doorway I had just entered and I feared a trap. My mind played a scenario: I enter the room, stepping past the closet accidentally, perhaps to look under the bed, perhaps to open the closet from the other side, and am shot dead from the closet. I heard the sound of voices behind me. From the other bedroom, "Clear!" From the living room, "Clear!" From the bathroom, "Clear!" From the kitchen, "Clear!" The bedroom was the last hiding place. It was all coming down to this moment. I would slide the closet door open and then? *Then what? This is what my life was worth? My entire life depended on what happened here — the sled run I'd made at the top of my street during winter, the years of soccer, the months training on the Olympic Development Teams, the philosophy papers I'd written at Vandy, the girlfriends I'd cried over, the dreams I still had. All of it was riding on the next second as I slid back the closet door.*

The realization was too horrible to comprehend. Not that it was happening. Rather, that I was about to trade in everything I'd ever known and loved, and everything I would ever know and love, to catch this unknown criminal. Why? To get a medal? Because it was my job? Because someone had to? No. To make sure criminals knew that, no matter how insane they got, no matter how fucked up they were, no matter what suicidal thing they decided to do, there was always going to be a couple of guys more insane, more fucked up, and more suicidal coming for them. There is a quieting of the heart and mind when you give up on life. I'm not sure if, at that moment, I truly gave up on everything or just reassigned value to everything. The first value was no longer preservation of existence. I wanted to punish, to match wills. I wanted to hunt down someone to let them know they weren't going to make it far enough. I wanted to suck into my blackness any light they had left, any hope for any outcome. I wanted to look anyone or anything in the eye and say, "I won." I wanted to die in place of any other cop. That action would be snatching victory from death and proclaiming, "You have tried to take someone who wasn't ready. I have replaced them. I am ready. I win."

I knew from my undercover days that I was going to die in this job. I could not leave and let these other cops ruin themselves in this danger, knowing what was happening to me was happening to them. I had made the decision to give up my dreams and my life. That decision had broken me. Now I was taking it a step further: I was giving up on my own survival. I was doing more than readying myself for death. I was pledging myself to The Reaper: *Come take me, here I stand.*

I slid the closet door open, and that's when the shotgun blast
caused me to throw myself backward into the wall opposite the bed.
But I had seen inside! No one was there. Ceiling. Attic. There was an
attic entrance in the ceiling of the closet. I picked myself up and
scrambled back behind the door. This was check, not checkmate. We
called the SWAT team. In 1996, Metro Officer Terry Daniels went up
some drop-down stairs to talk to a supposedly nonviolent subject
hiding in an attic. As he ascended the stairs, he was shot and killed.
Since then, we had a smart standing rule: we don't do attics. So, we
made the proper tactical decision to have the SWAT team affect the
arrest. They gassed the attic into oblivion, entered through the smoke
and tear gas, and Dwayne got taken to jail—after he fell, a lot. He'd
been sitting at the top of the attic entry with a shotgun, assuming one
of us would try to come upstairs. Terry saved us that day, though he
would never know it. We didn't need to learn the attic lesson twice. It's
always good to learn from the past, to constantly analyze mistakes and
successes.

I don't know if anyone will truly remember the courage of that
day because nothing really happened. We played hide and seek in the
house and found Dwayne. Finally, he came quietly. But I remember. I

remember the decision point.

Chapter 15:

A Tipping Point

"Death twitches my ear;

'Live,' he says...

'I'm coming." — Virgil

May 2001, Nashville

I sat in the nurse's office awaiting the test results. For six

weeks, I'd been waiting to hear if I was going to die of AIDs. The year

was 1999 and AIDS was then, as now, a very scary disease with a death

sentence attached. I could hear my blood pounding and the valves in my heart opening and closing. I couldn't think. I couldn't breathe. I

didn't want to die this way. I already had had so many traumas,

though, that I was closed off. Of all the times I was assaulted, spat

upon, shot at, stabbed, threatened, and psychologically injured, this

time was the worst. It sealed away a part of me.

My first wife, Lisa, sat with me while we waited for the results.

We hadn't had intercourse in those six weeks in case I was HIV-

positive. If I was, I had planned on divorcing her. She didn't know

about my plans, but what else was I to do? I couldn't risk infecting her

and I had no desire to tie her to my death. I was twenty-six and

thinking about suicide for the first time. I couldn't imagine going

forward in my life if I was HIV-positive. I wasn't going to wither away

in a hospital and let my family watch the effect of what a miserable

choice I'd made when I went into law enforcement. Secretly, I knew

they were disappointed in me; they didn't understand my decision to

be a cop. If I allowed myself to die this way, shame and rage would

overwhelm me sooner than the virus.

How I would choose to end my life was a big decision. I'd been

thinking about the suicide Mike Goldman and I had dealt with some

years earlier when we'd found a man, naked, in a bathtub of warm, bloody water. Intellectually, bleeding out in a warm bath seemed a

good way to go. It was peaceful. Another option was blowing my

brains out, but I had seen the results of that multiple times on various

crime scenes. It was usually messy. Plus, God forbid, I could instead

turn myself into a vegetable. I had settled on pills, getting drunk, and

slashing my wrists vertically. I wasn't sure if I could slash myself, but I

thought if I pulled off all three, one of the methods would take me out.

I was standing on the blade of a knife and I knew that, in the

next several seconds, I would step off the blade or fall upon it. All I

could do was wait for the doctor and remember what had happened.

Six weeks earlier, when I turned the corner from an alley onto a side

street, I'd seen a man hit a crack whore. Obviously, hitting anyone,

even a crack whore, was a crime. Obviously, I was going to stop and

arrest this thug. I pulled up the car quickly, called myself out on the

radio, and jumped out while calling to the guy. The crack whore was

actually a transvestite who was decently large. The thug was mad. The

transvestite was screaming back at him. I was pretty sure what had

happened and why the thug was angry. Both were very high on crack

and shaking. I tried getting them to calm down when, in the blink of an

eye, the thug turned and attacked me. I punched him squarely and,

wise enough to already have had my OC/CS spray in my other hand,
sprayed the living Jesus out of him. I held him in the headlock and
glanced up to check on the transvestite. He was standing there, still
yelling. I used my front leg to sweep the legs of the thug I had in the
headlock and dropped him to the ground with the intention of
handcuffing him as quickly as possible. I thought I was relatively safe
insofar as I was rescuing the transvestite from the guy who'd assaulted
him. That perception was an error.

With my knee on the back of the thug, I jerked his arms up and
handcuffed him quickly. While snapping the handcuff on his second
wrist, just in time, I never saw the kick that hit me in the head. Dazed, I
was knocked off the thug. The transvestite jumped on top of me and
rained blows down on me. A vicious fight ensued. I was very aware I
needed to get control of this guy quickly or I was going to be knocked
unconscious. I also was very aware I needed to find an instant to get to
the radio mic on my shoulder.

The kick to my head had rocked me, though, and I was having
trouble getting my bearings. I grabbed him behind his head and pulled
his face down close, keeping him from hitting me near the face. I then
swung my left leg under his chest and kicked him in the chest and

away from me. As he fell backward with the momentum from my kick,
I rolled away and disengaged for a second. Knowing the dispatcher
knew where I was and recognized my voice, I keyed the microphone
on my shoulder and yelled, "Get me help! Get me help!" As I was
getting to my feet, a kick landed in my ribs: the handcuffed thug had
decided to try to knock me back down. I hit him in the face with all I
had, knocking him backward into the curb and sidewalk. When I
turned around, a fist slammed into my face, drawing blood from my
lips and mouth. A flurry of punches ensued. Both of us were bleeding
and the transvestite was yelling something over and over, but my
hearing was almost gone from the adrenaline and from being dizzy.

As I landed a good shot, I felt the transvestite's nose explode.
He lost his footing and I used the opportunity to crash into him,
knocking him to the ground. I landed on top of him. He flipped onto his
stomach to turn his face away from me and crawl forward. I was able
to spray him with the OC/CS but he was so high from the crack that the
spray had no effect. He was still yelling something over and over. His
face and hands were covered in blood, as was my nose and mouth.
When the spray didn't work, I slammed his face into the street and
grabbed his left hand, yanking it as hard as I could behind his back. I

slapped a handcuff on his left wrist, but I couldn't hold him as he twisted and rolled away. I was able to maintain control of the handcuff's empty side as we pulled and yanked each other. He was struggling to get away from me and I was pulling him back to the ground. When he spit blood in my eyes, I accidentally let go of the handcuff. He then struck me with the handcuff, slinging it like a weapon with one side attached to his wrist and one side free as a metal blade.

I could have used deadly force, but I knew I didn't have to kill him just yet. Jerking out my baton, I struck him several times in the head, opening bloody wounds. He reeled backward. My hearing came back just then and I heard what he was yelling: "Now you have AIDS, too! I gave you AIDS! Now you have AIDS!" I struck him again in the head, finally knocking him down and nearly unconscious. I finished handcuffing him as the other cars arrived and screeched to a stop.

The scene was awful. The first suspect was lying relatively quietly where he had crashed on the curb, still handcuffed and bleeding. The transvestite was fairly injured, covered in blood and, as a six-foot man in a bikini top and jean shorts, a ridiculous-looking mess. I, too, was covered in blood, panting hard, exhausted, and dizzy. As I got off the transvestite, I yelled to my friend Jason, "If he moves, kill

him!" I walked to the trunk of my car and got out a clean towel to wipe

blood from my face and arms. I then leaned over and puked,

remembering the blood and spit from the transvestite hitting my face.

The ambulance came and took him to the hospital. I didn't need to go.

My lips and mouth were cut, bruised, and swollen, but nothing too bad.

The paramedics cleaned me up, and I went home.

The next day, a complaint awaited me. A black female officer,

who was forced to leave the force years later for various infractions,

had reported me to Internal Affairs because of what I'd said to Jason:

"If he moves, kill him!" I had to write various reports and supplements

outlining my use of force, per any use of force, but I also had to explain

my "unprofessional statement to another officer requesting the use of

deadly force should the suspect fail to further comply while

handcuffed."

So there I was, sitting in the doctor's office, six weeks from that

day, too scared and desperate to feel the anger and rage that had

ripped through me. This piece-of-shit, crazy crackhead was going to

ruin everything I'd ever wanted to be and everything I was ever going

to do. Plus, the argument between the thug and the transvestite was over a twenty-dollar crack rock, found in the left front pocket of the transvestite during a search. That's what my life was worth on this day. That was the measurement. When I stood before God and he weighed my life in his hands, he would ask me to step upon Golden Scales. On the other side of the scales would not be The Book of Life, where all the names of the saved are written. On the other side of the scales would not be two angels, one telling of all my good deeds, and the other arguing for my purity of heart. On the other side of the scales would not be Jesus Christ, welcoming me and saying, "I have died so you may live." No. On the other side of the scales would be the thing for which I had given my life— "a chalk-like substance which based upon my professional opinion resembled crack cocaine," as I'd told the court hundreds of times before.

The doctor walked out, stood before me, and smiled. The results were negative. I swallowed my suicide plans. I tried to swallow down my pain and anger, too, but I couldn't. I couldn't believe in a world where my life could become worth so little so fast. I couldn't believe in a God that would allow the kind of suffering I was feeling inside. The suffering was growing like a cancer and I couldn't keep swallowing incident after incident, morbid murder scene after violent confrontation. I was full. Was I to thank God for this salvation? If this whole thing was God's doing, then I'll spit his pity right back in his face and I'll say, *Fuck you, God. I won't allow you to measure me anymore.*

The boy was crippled with pain. The wolf walked forward and went back into uniform and onto the street. The wolf didn't need God.

Chapter 16:

The Way It Is

No one but me can save myself, but it's too late

Now I can't think, think why I should even try

— Metallica, "Fade to Black"

July 2001, Nashville

The Nations was a conglomerate of shithole houses with state

street names such as Alabama Street and Dakota Street. I can't

describe 5599 Michigan because I can only see it now in grays and darkness in my mind. There will be no color for me in that memory

again. It was a ranch house with a single-car driveway and a single-car

garage set back from the house. The row of three garage windows was

broken long ago: jagged pieces of glass still jutted from the frames. The

garage was filled with old furniture, lawn mowers, bags of garbage,

and mountains of old beer cans. The house was in no better shape,

save for the unbroken windows. The gutters hung from the roof. The

lawn was a mishmash of gravel and weeds. The call to 911 had come

from a neighbor's son, a boy of fourteen who lived across the street

from 5599 Michigan. The call was dispatched as a 10-54PE, which

came across the radio like this, "Attention all cars, all cars, 10-54PE in

Progress. Emergency, 5594 Michigan Ave. Caller is 14-year-old

juvenile who states his neighbor is coming over to kill his father.

Unknown if suspect has arrived or is armed. Closest cars respond Code

3 Emergency. Time is 2155 hours."

Really, The Nations was nothing more than a small back street

and alley by the Preston Taylor projects where my gang unit was

working. I was at the address in under thirty seconds, assuming I was

about to find (a) a bullshit call, (b) myself in a gunfight with the

neighbor, or (c) a dead neighbor and distraught fourteen-year-old caller. The silence was eerie when I got out of my car. I should have grabbed my shotgun, but calls like this went out all day and all night in the ghettoes. As I walked up the driveway, keeping away from the line of fire of the open front door, I observed someone carrying a shotgun out of the open front door, right on cue. For probably the first time in my career, I actually yelled, "Police! Freeze! Do not move or I will shoot you! Freeze right now! Do not move your gun or you die." I articulated and said all that in as calm a voice as I could muster because the last thing I needed was this guy jumping, turning the shotgun toward me, and saying, "What?" as his last word. Or, as is so often said in the South, "Do what?" The suspect was a paradigm of white trash, complete with stained wife beater tank top, overhanging gut, never-washed tobacco-stained jeans, and no shoes.

"You are going to hold that shotgun with your left hand by the barrel, place your right hand over your head, and lower that gun with your left hand to the ground," I said. "If you turn toward me a single inch, I will empty this whole magazine into you, clear?" He did as he was told. When the shotgun was on the ground, he walked toward me, as ordered, and got on the ground, face down. I handcuffed him without incident. I was certain I had arrived here having to deal with

(c) a dead neighbor and distraught fourteen-year-old caller. But out came both the neighbor and the juvenile. They had hidden themselves in a closet and waited for the police to come take drunken Wyatt Earp with the shotgun to jail. We did. But drunken Wyatt Earp had something to say along the way about where he lived at 5599 Michigan, across the street. As soon as Matt and I booked dumbass into jail, we drove right back to 5599 Michigan.

We banged on the door, knowing everyone should be sound asleep since it was close to midnight at that point. Carl Miller came to the door wearing dirty jeans and a white stained tee shirt. He was about forty-five years old, five foot six, and one hundred forty pounds with gray hair in a mullet and a very unkempt gray mustache. Surprised to see us, he quickly stepped outside, which is always a warning about something going on inside.

"Sir, are you alone in the house?" I asked.

"Ah, yeah," he said. "No one here but me."

"Sir, you been drinking?"

"Yeah, but ain't drove none," he said. "It's my house."

"Sir, you better tell me right now if you have someone else in this house," I said, "because I'm going to look, and when and if I find someone else, we are going to have a real problem."

Now normally we, as police, wouldn't have the right to enter this guy's house without his permission or a search warrant, neither of which we were going to get. But we could enter if we believed someone was being held against his or her will, a domestic was occurring, or there'd been a 911 hang up from the house phone. In this case, we had reason to believe a child might be in danger, and most cops will tell you, off the record, that if we have reason to believe a child may be in danger, we are coming in and you can go fuck yourself. That was the case in this instance. So we patted down Carl Miller for weapons and pushed past him into his house.

The small living room was the first room in the house. It contained a TV, which was on, against the right wall, a couch against the back wall, and a chair across from the TV. On the couch was a naked boy, no more than twelve. The boy didn't talk, couldn't really talk. He made sounds. The boy was bruised near his hips and butt. Homosexual pornography magazines and VHS tapes were scattered around the floor and near the TV. Several beer cans were on the floor and a side table. The relationship between the boy and Carl was quite

clear.

"Explain this," I said, in a quiet voice. Carl's fucked-up mind

couldn't come up with a lot.

"The boy loves me and I love him," he said, adding that he took

care of the boy, whose mother had died of a drug overdose. We called

for Youth Services on the radio, handcuffed Carl, got the boy a blanket,

and waited. I swallowed again and again as I stood there, choking on

something I could feel was stuck. I was rejecting what I was seeing. Yet

the reality—what I came to call the third reality—was searing itself

into me yet again. I'd been here before.

The longer I was in law enforcement, the more I realized the

complete disconnect between the three realities, or worlds, I was so

struggling to reconcile. The reality most of us grow up with is a faith in

the social contract by which we live. In order for our society to work,

we all agree to a kind of Hobbesian social contract in which we

exchange certain individual freedoms for certain guarantees of other

freedoms. For Instance, our society doesn't allow vigilantism. Instead,

we use the police to catch criminals. Without the police, we would live, as Thomas Hobbes, a seventeenth-century British political philosopher, said, in a natural state of individuals not cohering into a society—"solitary, poor, nasty, brutish and short." Such a state would not permit a civilized society: self-interest would rule and there would be no rights or contracts governing behavior. Life would be anarchic, that is, without leadership or even the concept of sovereignty. Individuals in such a chaotic state of nature would be apolitical and asocial, always choosing to take what they needed through might, rather than any sense of value or reasoned action. In such a chaotic state, humans are always at war and are unable to grow or enlighten themselves. We now have laws to govern everything from dog licenses to cybercrime. Our social contract is constantly adapting to keep us all safe and in a state of cooperation. You and every other citizen who is not a cop or a soldier are all in a giant circle surrounded by wagons. When something bad happens, we consider the occurrence a tragedy, an accident, an unlucky incident. Some criminal broke through the circled wagons and fucked something up.

The second reality is the one outside the wagons. It is the base, disgusting, animalistic, anarchic world where might makes right and there truly are no mechanisms in place to govern, protect, or enforce.

That reality is one the average citizen doesn't see, and that was a tough reality for me, I admit, but one I could understand, thrive in, and react to, at least philosophically. I could justify myself as a bringer of consequences, or even simply one seeking vengeance for wronged victims. I knew I could muster the courage to enforce something if the system as a whole followed through on the social contract: The prosecutors would get a conviction. The public would be duly outraged at the crime, and the police would know that risking their lives was worth the cost. Everyone marched to the same ethical drumbeat and expected those who fell out of line to be brought back in line. I could handle that.

One evening when I turned the corner behind a row of housing projects while trying to sneak up on a crack dealer, I saw the angriest human I'd ever seen squared off to fight two women. Roland James had his fists clinched and was as mad at his grandma and aunt as a ten-year-old could get.

"Whoa! Whoa!" I said, smiling from ear to ear and looking at Roland's four-foot bowling ball frame. His lips stuck out in a pout. "What's going on here?"

"Ro Ro wants to go to the carnival with the big kids up on Twenty-eighth," his grandma said, "and he's not old enough, so he's gotta stay here with me and his Auntie and he don't like it one bit!"

"Ro Ro?" I asked. "You aren't sassing or back talking your Gram, are you?"

"No! I ain't sassing her!" he said. "I'm old enough to go. I'm ten years old! She won't let me 'cause she's afraid I'll get hurt, but I won't get hurt. She's being unfair and stupid!"

"Ro Ro!" his aunt shouted. "Don't you tell Gram-mama she' stupid! See, Mr. Police, he's sassing and back talking. Go on and take him to jail." She couldn't help but laugh. Ro Ro was a sight. How anyone could be mad at this boy was beyond me. He was so puffed up with his chest out, it made his little round shape look even rounder. He was obviously conscious of being short, but puffing up just made him look hysterical.

"Ro Ro, you can't talk back to your aunt or your Gram," I said. "How about you come with me in the police car and I buy you an ice cream at Dairy Queen? You have to be ten years old to go, though, or you aren't old enough. How old did you say you were, again?"

"I'm ten! That's old enough to go! Can I go, Gram?" he asked. Then he turned to me, wary, "You ain't gonna take me to jail, are you?"

"Nope. No jail. Only to the Dairy Queen and back," I said. "You can turn on the lights and siren, too, but you have to obey your Gram and Auntie about this carnival and give up arguing with them, OK?"

"Deal!" Ro Ro suddenly was the happiest a little ball of kid could be.

"Where's his mom?" I asked Ro Ro's grandmother while he went to put on a shirt.

"She's never around, always in jail, doing drugs," she said. "I been taking care of him since he was born."

"OK, well, we will be back in about twenty-five minutes," I said. "You don't mind?"

"No, that's nice of you," she replied. "Ro Ro will talk about this for days."

Ro Ro came running out and, as promised, I took him to Dairy Queen for a cone. I let him play with the sirens and lights, too. He was all smiles. After that, Ro Ro became my little buddy. He would wave and say hi when he saw me or my car. For Christmas that year, my wife

and I bought him a Sony PlayStation with some games.

"Just like the older kids have!" he crowed. Every month or two,

I checked on Ro Ro, making sure he was trying hard in school, staying

out of fights and trouble, and helping his aunt and grandmother.

Because so much hatred was directed at me, and the police in general,

in the ghetto, it felt nice being able to reach out with something other

than a cold wall of defense. I felt like I could send out some caring and

support from inside the wall before I had to close it back up. That

release did more for me than anything I was doing for Ro Ro.

He grew older. I was transferred into and out of Narcotics, but I

ended up back in his area before long. By the time Ro Ro was twelve

years old, he wouldn't wave or say hi if he was with other boys. I

understood and didn't begrudge him. Who knows what was being

said? Besides, preteens are the greatest conformists on earth. I would

still stop by his house, bring him a Christmas gift or an Easter basket—

Ro Ro loved chocolate and never outgrew his belly —to make sure he

knew I was there if he ever needed help. I never really spoke much

again with his aunt, save for the occasional hello. His grandmother

would let me know about his school and if he got into any trouble.

When Ro Ro was thirteen, his family moved to a different housing area. I was worried about this though, supposedly, they had more family there. Besides, geographically, the John Henry Hale project was literally five minutes away. By that time, Ro Ro wouldn't acknowledge me at all in public, but he would talk and joke with me if I caught him at home. He was getting all C's in school, and I was impressed and happy with that. He actually showed me his report card one Christmas Day. He was proud of his work, which was a great sign for his future. Ro Ro was excited about high school because he was going to play defense line "just like Jevon Kearse," the Tennessee Titan's star defensive lineman known in the NFL as "The Freak." Ro Ro said he was the next "Freak." I told him he better start training and stop eating. He laughed and reminded me how good his grandmother's cooking was. He was on his way out of the ghetto. By fourteen, Ro Ro was off and running.

When the call went out, it sounded like this: "Attention all West cars, all West cars, 10-52PE, shooting in progress, at the dead end horseshoe of John Henry Hale, 17th Ave North and Jo Johnson. Multiple shots fired. Caller now reports several people shot. Fire and Medical notified, Any West car in the area respond. Code 3 Emergency. Time is

2355 hrs." I was thirty seconds away at the time. Grabbing my shotgun, I exited my vehicle and ran toward where I had heard shots. People started pointing. With the lights around us still dim from having been shot out, the only real light came from some porches and my flashlight. Near the playground, in an alley between apartment buildings, was a body.

The second reality, the one outside the wagons, is filled with brutality and violence, yes. But deep inside it lies a third reality — the darkest place of all. In the third reality, the darkness is devastating because you don't see it coming, and when it comes, its blackness is suffocating. It's the place where the system just doesn't reach or has so completely failed that the result is unacceptable, even unfathomable. The outrage in the third reality is so intense because the very concept of "value" has been abnegated. It is not a place beyond good and evil. It is a place where evil has the same value as good, and either outcome is acceptable because the process has so completely broken down.

The goal of law enforcement is to serve and protect the community. Law enforcement officers (and certainly soldiers, firefighters, and others) are willing to give their lives in the process of serving and protecting because they believe in the value of human life.

They believe in the value of keeping the social contract functioning so society can be a safe place for people. A sacrificed life has meaning only in the context of a society that values life. If it does not, it can't ask us to risk our lives for its sake.

In the third reality, though, society has turned its back because of ignorance, politics, or choice when it prioritizes problems to solve. In this place of darkness, society does not have the means to protect the innocent and so the worst kind of tragedy — preventable tragedy — strikes. To us law enforcement officers, to soldiers, to all those sheepdogs keeping watch over the flocks everywhere in this country, there is no priority greater than protecting human life and stopping preventable tragedy. So the third reality is the place where we are morally ripped to shreds, because we trusted that you, society, you, those in power, and you, those who asked us to give our lives, would not ask us to do so in vain.

Simply put, the third reality is where those in power betray what's right, giving you no reason not to betray it yourself. In The Nations that night, we couldn't take the boy from Carl. He wasn't so drunk that he couldn't take care of the boy, who was in Carl's custody since his mother had died of a drug overdose several years earlier. The boy's eighty-year-old grandmother came over with some legal documents to help straighten things out. After Youth Services left, Matt and I sat outside Carl's house, leaning against our cars, speechless and outraged. Legally, there was nothing we could prove. Legally, we had no direct evidence. But Carl was fucking guilty and it was all over his face, the boy's face, the bruises on the boy's body, and the circumstantial evidence all around the shithole house. It was not acceptable to me to leave a pedophile in his house to rape a boy, and that was that.

Sam and I may have gone back into that house. We may have taken Carl behind the house. We may have made sure it was going to be a long time before Carl could do much of anything. We may have done a lot of things. But one thing we did not do was leave a pedophile in his house to rape a boy, at least not that night.

That's how you start to police after seeing nothing happen time and time again. You start believing that no one cares about what's right, and the lesson that stands the truest is that evil wins because it simply does more damage than good. Good can try to paint a room a better color, but evil just drops a hand grenade and blows the whole goddamned place to splinters. You learn that there are no rules and that the third reality exists anywhere anyone takes a moral stand.

Eventually, you realize the bullies will never stop, no matter the rule of

law, no matter the ethical system, no matter the morality of the action.

So you start punching back. You hit and you hit. At first you regret it,

and then you hit harder. You punch everyone right in the fucking

mouth as hard as you can, as many times as you can, because as long as

you are hitting someone, anyone, they are not hurting someone else.

Still, you can't win, and that's the final lesson. Evil wins because it's

chaos and you can't recognize the pattern because there isn't one.

Evil won the night I saw the body between the rows of

apartment housing. I was too late to do anything. From ten feet away, I

knew who it was. I dropped to my knees and rolled him over, looking

for some sign of life. I checked for a pulse and found none. There was a

lot of blood on the ground and I knew Ro Ro was dead. My heart would

have broken if it could have. Instead, rage and anger, my old friends,

plugged the hole pain had ripped open. I hunched over Ro Ro with my

hand resting against my forehead. *Why care about anything at all? This*

was how it was, God? This is who gets shot? How can I reach out again,

ever? Doesn't matter.

Chapter 17:
My Vest: Part II

Growing darkness taking dawn

I was me, but now he's gone

— Metallica, "Fade to Black"

Summer 2001, Nashville

My vest was no longer itchy. Baby powder and a shaved chest – those were the keys. I never removed the right shoulder strap. I just unvelcroed the two black chest straps and slid the vest over my head. I also knew exactly how much to tighten the straps. The blue vest had faded from a royal blue into a lighter shade with some white salt stains permanently seared into the fabric by the chest. It had even molded

itself near my stomach to where it hit my belt and the ASP baton,

holster, and radio antenna. It was comfortable, though hot, in the

summer Southern heat and humidity. But if you get shot at a couple of

times, you won't take it off. Trust me.

It wasn't comfortable like a good friend, though. It was more

like the muted memory of an ex-girlfriend you truly loved but who left

you sad. My vest was now my lifeboat and my last will and testament.

I'd had a small holster for a 5-shot .38 revolver sewn into the left side.

Everyone I knew carried a backup gun and most who worked in the

projects carried a third gun. The thinking was that you could use your

left hand to reach what you wore on your ankle if you couldn't use

your right or if someone was on top of you trying to take your gun

from your right holster. If you had to use your right hand and couldn't

get to your ankle or your primary gun, you went for the one in your

vest.

Like I said, my vest was a lifeboat for a last-ditch attempt to

survive, and life can disappear pretty fast. There was a day, for

instance, when, at 10:44 p.m., everyone was alive. At 10:45 p.m., they

were all dead.

I was sitting in my police car in the parking lot of a car wash across from a set of projects near an interstate. It was 10:44 p.m. and my shift was over in one minute. I was poised to jump on that interstate and head home. Just then, I heard tires squeal and saw two pairs of headlights fly around a corner and head toward my car wash. As the cars came nearer, the sound of gunfire was unmistakable: pop, pop, pop, pop, pop, pop. It was clear the first car had seen me and was trying to get to me, while the second car was chasing the first. Two thugs were leaning out the windows, firing weapons at the first car. Orange flames darted from the barrels with each shot.

I yelled into the radio, "Shots fired, 40th and Charlotte!" and jumped out of my car, fearing they'd both crash into me and trap me inside during a gunfight. As I sought shelter behind a concrete wall, the first car squealed to a stop in the car wash lot directly in front of my car. The second car turned north on Charlotte, clearly seeking the same interstate I'd been eyeing a moment earlier. A Metro police car flew after it, but not close enough to immediately engage the vehicle. I could only hope it would narrow the distance before the interstate took the vehicle out of eyesight. I turned toward the vehicle stopped near me and ordered everyone out at gunpoint, still very unsure of what was happening. A young girl, about twenty, jumped out of the

driver seat and screamed that she and her boyfriend were shot. I

pulled rubber gloves from my pocket and threw them at her, yelling

for her to sit and use them to cover her wound, while I approached the

vehicle very guardedly. I yelled at the front passenger seat occupant, a

young male, to show me his hands. He just stared at me, blinking

every once in a while.

I risked a glance to the backseat and saw another young male,

unconscious and slumped against the window. I remember thinking,

Jesus Christ, what the fuck? I ripped open the door of the front

passenger vehicle and, yelling for the kid not to move, grabbed a gun

from the floorboard by his foot. I holstered my gun, quickly cleared

the other gun ammo, and threw it to the ground. I yanked the

passenger out of the backseat and onto the ground. I ripped open his

shirt. He was dead. Multiple gunshot exit wounds were visible through

his chest. The male in the passenger front seat was going unconscious.

The girl, the driver, came around to the passenger side, crying for her

boyfriend. That's when the front seat passenger began convulsing. I

grabbed him out of the front seat and pulled him to the ground, where

he went into cardiac arrest. I tried to start CPR on him, but he was just dying. It was hopeless. Everything was hopeless, and everyone was dying. I yelled in my radio again for an ambulance.

Jumping up, I turned toward the girl and pulled her hands away from her right shoulder where she was shot. It was a minor wound, thank God, and I gave her a wad of gauze and told her to use it, instead of the gloves. I had to make sure that she was going to live, that someone here was going to live. The backseat passenger, her boyfriend, had no pulse, so I returned to the front seat passenger. He, too, had no pulse and was dead. I tried CPR again, to no avail. All of that happened in about ninety seconds.

I knew my death would come like that—lying on the street, looking up at someone. When I got home that night, I wrote my blood type on the back and front of my vest with a Sharpie. I placed a picture of my family inside, where the metal shock plate slides into a pocket near the heart. I also taped a poem to the outside along with instructions to read it at my funeral. I was certain I was going to die and I wanted everyone to know that my death was OK with me — expected, foreseen, and, to some extent, welcomed. I was in too many dangerous situations every day and the odds were simple: no one survives everything.

Then I taped to the front of my vest the last lines of "Lament," the song Eva Perón sings as she is dying in *Evita*, the movie starring Madonna and Antonio Banderas. Eva (Madonna) is lying in her bed, dying, and singing about her choice— to burn like a bright fire, or live longer. She sings of how a year in her youth felt like forever. The song ends with her final thought about her choice to shine bright instead of long:

> *And how I lived, how they shone*
>
> *But how soon the lights were gone*

That was how I felt. I was shining bright but had completely given up on having a future, on living. I knew I'd given up too much. I knew the wolf had grown stronger than the boy. I knew the wolf was killing me.

Remember the old allegory about the frog in boiling water? That's what happened to me. If you put a frog in a pot of room temperature water and turn up the heat quickly, the water boils, and the frog, sensing its own demise, leaps from the water. But if, instead, you slowly turn up the heat, increasing the water's temperature little by little, the frog will not recognize the danger until it's too late. It will die. Or maybe it's more like playing chess against a master. There's a point when you're done, even if you don't know it. Just because you

don't know the game is over, doesn't mean it isn't over.

The abrupt slash and assault on my life and soul during the

bank robber shooting started a slow simmering heat of anger and

sadness that culminated one night at the Rio Bravo on West End

Avenue, a place that had been one of my favorite Vanderbilt hangouts.

Rio Bravo was *the* place to go for great margaritas and everyone's

place for Cinco de Mayo. In college at Vandy, Eli, Ian, Grayson, and I

went to Rio Bravo quite often. Eli and I used to get the steak with an

awesome green salsa. Since the place was in the shadow of Vanderbilt

Stadium, it was easy walking distance to fraternity row and our

favorite bars. Cinco de Mayo nights were fun. In Nashville, May 5

usually is fairly hot. By then, everyone has shed winter clothing and

there are colored banners everywhere. The bartender blared a whistle

while pouring tequila shots from a bandolier slung around her chest as

if she was a Mexican bandito with ammunition. The green, white, and

red of the Mexican flag were draped all around the bar and parking

lot. Usually, we'd have to wait in line in the lot – but, lo and beyond,

another bartender señorita with tequila shots was whooping it up with

a whistle outside, too.

But this night was not that Cinco de Mayo night. This time was

not that Vanderbilt time. This time, it was raining and late at night.

Vice had set up a deal with a guy for fourteen thousand Ecstasy pills,

and he was going to meet the Undercover, a.k.a. the Duck, in the

parking lot. The guy sat there in a black Ford. Andrew moved in first in

his police car and tried to box in the guy's vehicle from the right.

Myself and the rest of the Take- down Team pulled our cars in tight,

trying to use the vehicles as obstacles to keep the suspect from fleeing.

We all jumped out of our cars. I leapt out and started toward the

suspect vehicle while drawing my Glock. The guy slammed his car

forward. The sounds of metal crunching, an engine revving, and tires

burning pierced the night through the rain. I moved in with the

takedown team, on foot, to arrest the guy, as he slammed into other

cars in the lot in a desperate attempt to run down Andrew and another

officer. We opened fire, killing him.

That shooting was different because it was calculated as a

possible outcome. It seemed like we approached a vehicle hundreds of

times—sometimes in plain clothes, sometimes in raid gear, sometimes

in uniform, sometimes in a parking lot, sometimes in a garage,

sometimes on a traffic stop. Always, you have your gun drawn in case the guy tries to shoot you or run you over. That almost happens more frequently than you'd think. So this shooting was less painful, more numbing. I don't even know if I hit him. I fired four rounds.

There is a moment from that night that is frozen in my mind's eye: I see Andrew standing in the lot, diagonally across from me, on the driver's side of his car. He's situated in front of his car's headlight. I see the rain frozen in the light from the headlight, though it's blurry because my focus is on him. I see his Glock 27 compact in the front of his tactical belt. He uses that for a backup weapon. He has his larger Glock aimed in. He cants his body when the driver moves forward to run over him/someone/everyone. My vision switches, like another snapshot, to the driver, brown haired, gaze straight ahead. I see into the front passenger side of his car. I look past the side mirror. I can't hear anything but I know Andrew is firing. I can almost hear the pops. In the vision, I am removed. I watch my Glock fire from about four feet away. Other people had made the same decision. The threat of death isn't so great to me. I fire in self-defense because I don't want to get run over, either, but more in defense of the first two officers.

I will never forget sitting in the rain that night, looking at Rio Bravo and thinking about how my life had changed since Vanderbilt and how unrecognizable I was to myself and those around me. That

night, I knew I was no longer me. I stared at Vanderbilt and then back

to Rio Bravo. I thought about Cinco De Mayo. As the rain fell, I tried to

remember what I used to feel like back at Vandy, when I wasn't me, or,

maybe, when I was.

Chapter 18:

A Proud Sheepdog

A hero is somebody who voluntarily walks into the unknown.

- Tom Hanks

September 2001, Nashville

By 10 a.m. on September 11, 2001, all police officers in Nashville had been called in to work, just in case. Randy and I were watching the news, like everyone else, when we realized we'd better turn on our radios and get dressed. From the standpoint of police in another city, we had our own action plans for various emergencies, but none applied to 9/11. I'm sure the brass at headquarters in downtown Nashville sent quite a few more officers to the airport. My West FLEX unit was deployed to be visible in and around the downtown area. Traffic was as light as it is on holidays. The country was scared and in front of the TV. As I jumped in my police car and Randy jumped in his, we both hit the blue lights and swooped in different directions, me to West FLEX, him to South Precinct. Other blue lights in the area screamed toward downtown. We had a million questions when our West FLEX sergeant arrived, but he had as little information as everyone else did. So we just drove around to be seen and, somehow, reassure the public.

Watching the brave cops and firefighters of the NYPD, Port Authority PD, and FDNY rush into the burning towers, and then watching as the towers fell on them, was heartbreaking for all Americans. For me, the tragic loss of so many heroes in uniform crystallized what I had come to believe would be the end of my life — dying in the line of duty, wearing my uniform, trying to win. My mother called me that day. To her, the loss of so many emergency personnel was one more reason her son should never have gone into law enforcement. She was very fond of telling me why I should leave

the field, sometimes using the tactic of reminding me how "smart" I

was and how "successful" I would be if I changed occupations. Other

times, she would try in ways she believed to be subtle—informing me

of all the "important" jobs my old friends from Kansas City were doing.

"So-and-So is a doctor," she would say. "Can you believe it? You

were always so much smarter than her. And So-and-So just got a job at

that prestigious law firm you always wanted to work at downtown.

You could have had that job. You were always so much better than him

at everything. And can you believe So-and-So? She and her husband,

So-and-So, started a business and are so rich now. You shouldn't have

gone to Vanderbilt if you wanted to waste your time as a police officer.

You could have gone to any school. Why don't you get a law degree like

So-and-So? He didn't go to nearly as good a school."

I think that, mostly, her suggestions came from a good place.

Mom wanted me to be successful and have the freedom that money

buys. She wanted me to stop living in constant danger of losing my

life and not be a miserable wretch of a human who hated all other

humans. But part of her really hated that I was "just a cop" while her

friends' sons were now "surpassing" her perfect son in terms of money and status. On a couple of days later that month, out of frustration,

anger, and fear for my safety (love), she called me a "lowly cop." I was

certain I would die in the line of duty. I wanted to go out like a hero,

and I was going to be goddamned if my own mother was going to

detract from what I saw as my ultimate gift to humanity —my life —

by denying glory and honor to those who gave their lives in such a

heroic manner. I wrote her back this email:

> *Tuesday, 9-18-01*
>
> *Mom, last night I was amazed and stunned at some of
> the things that you said in our phone conversation. At
> the time, I could not speak my mind appropriately
> enough to respond because I was so hurt at the things
> that you said and so ashamed of you for saying them.*
>
> *We talked about all the events which have transpired
> since Tuesday.*
>
> *President Bush said the bravery of the police officers in
> New York is "seared in the national consciousness." But
> you said, "Bet you wish you were in the FBI and could be
> investigating terrorism."*
>
> *You said the comment with the obvious intention of
> making me wish I was in the FBI instead of a police
> officer in Nashville. For if I was an FBI agent, I would get
> to travel to New York and help in the exciting*

*investigation which is commencing in the exciting area
of terrorism. I would get to pursue those responsible, and
those who would yet be responsible, and bring them to
justice. How satisfying, how "noble," and how
prestigious. Wouldn't it be neat for you to be able to tell
people that your son, the Special Agent, was
investigating the terrorist incident? Wouldn't that make
you feel important and successful? Yes, and you would
have missed the entire lesson which the nation has
learned this week, and is just now appreciating for
probably the first time ever. Who is the nation
celebrating? Who is the nation calling "heroes"? Who are
being given special burials, having their efforts
applauded and death toll read every five minutes on the
news? Who ran into the buildings when everyone was
running out?*

*The New York police officers and firefighters, that's who.
Ten percent of the victims were police officers and
firefighters. They are the heroes. Sure, few may have
been businessmen or lawyers, and none were
congressman, senators, or mayors. The lowly silver–
shielded police were the ones who died.*

*They are the heroes. Do you know why? Because they did
more than their job required and more than anyone
dreamed. As people ran out of the buildings, they ran in.
They ran up the stairs as people ran down. They could
have stood outside the trade centers and assisted all*

those coming out. They could have helped seal off the area with tape. They could have stayed outside and they could have then lived. But they didn't. They choose to try. And they died.

And they probably didn't save a single person.

But the lowly police officers (and firefighters) are being called heroes because they showed exactly what the ideal qualities of a human being are. They didn't list them, teach them, write about them, or point them out. They exhibited them. They died by them.

Guess where I would have been had that tragedy happened in Nashville? Guess what I would have done? Guess if I would be here today? I hope if I am ever confronted with such a decision that I can bravely act as those police officers did. I know I would. I have been a hero before and I probably will be again. But never could I imagine having to act as those police did. Did you not think that they knew as they entered the buildings that they would not come out?

My fellow officers and I have talked about this because we recognize that such a scenario is possible. But we never once, NOT ONCE, wish we were a bystander on the scene. We wished, rather, that we had been able to run into the trade center, too, meeting our destiny, but trying to save someone. Because we are the few who have the ability and courage to try.

*This nation, this week, is as proud of the police as I have
always been. They are thankful that we are here and
were there. You should be, too. And you should be
prouder, this week above all other weeks, to tell people
that I am a police officer. Because while some wish they
were FBI in Nashville on Tuesday, no one wishes they
were a police officer in New York on Tuesday. No one
wishes they were an officer but us "lowly police officers"
who saw the bravest of our brothers die the bravest
death, mourn them like family, and thusly would have
traded places with them in a heartbeat.*

*If you cannot be proud of me this week, you cannot be
proud of me ever, in any endeavor.*

I love you, Ryan

In Mom's defense, I had overreacted to her email and she
immediately explained what she had meant and how much she loved
me. But she hated me being a cop. That never changed. And how could
it? I was destroying her son.

When I found this email, about twelve years later, four major
things struck me.

First, I was struck by how desperate I was to define myself as a
hero and be recognized as one. I had needed to be celebrated for what

I was doing because I was certain I was going to give up my life doing it. I saw my mother's statement that I was a "lowly police officer" as a denial of my life's work. To me, still, police work is noble and glorious. We fight real evil and help bring about real justice. Anyone who didn't agree with my belief was denying the validity of my life, and I wasn't having that. I needed people to see the insane life I was living, and to acknowledge I was dying inside to live it. I needed the world to stop, point at the police, and say, "Jesus Christ, how do you guys and gals do it? You are amazing! Thank you!" All of America was doing just that! Sadly, we all know, despite the "Never Forget" stickers and slogans, so much of the public has indeed forgotten a great deal of the loss and sacrifice of that day. Without a doubt, the public also has forgotten the continued sacrifice of law enforcement and firefighters around the country.

Second, in my constant state of anger, frustration, and my certainty that I would die in the line of duty, I punish my mother with promises that I would, if given the chance, run into a burning building. I used to punish my family with stories. I would tell them story after story about the horrible things that happened to me, that I saw, that I had to do, and I would tell them until they couldn't take anymore. I knew they weren't going to die the death of the soul that I was suffering, but I wanted to cut them so they could feel a little of the pain.

Third, I wrote, "But the lowly police officers (and firefighters) are being called heroes. Because they showed exactly what the ideal qualities of a human being are. They didn't list them, teach them, write about them, or point them out. They exhibited them. They died by them." This little paragraph is interesting and provides insight into what I was thinking. The police "showed exactly what the ideal qualities of a human being are." What were those qualities? To be willing to die for the job, perhaps? Willing to trade one's own life for another's based on a one-for-one principle, and not a value judgment. No parent can do that. No parent could trade their child's life for a random person's life. But I thought it so very noble to trade my life for that of another human being because I was certain I would indeed die by that exchange, I could not imagine a greater, nobler action. I was trying to make my upcoming death hold value.

Fourth, I again separate intentions and actions. I assign zero value to words about the "ideal qualities of a human being." I also assign less value to those who teach, write about, or point out "the ideal qualities of a human being" than I do to cops and those anywhere who exhibit those qualities and die by executing them. In essence, I am no longer debating intentions versus results or means versus ends. Rather, I have made it very clear that I perceive no more gray in the world. There are those individuals and actions for whom and for which the end has positive results—me and most hard-working cops—and there are those individuals and actions for whom and for which the end has negative results—criminals. Finally, there are those individuals who "list, teach, debate, write about, and criticize ends," preferring the gray and simple area of intentions over the difficult and dangerous execution of action. That is to say, my worldview had become narrowed: there were three types of people—sheepdogs, wolves, and sheep.

Lt. Col. Dave Grossman (RET) wrote an essay entitled "On Sheep, Wolves, and Sheepdogs" that appears in his book *On Combat: The Psychology and Physiology of Deadly Conflict in War and in Peace* . It's amazing how parallel my thinking, exemplified by my letter to my mom, had become to Grossman's psychological postulates on those who live in violence:

> *If you have no capacity for violence then you are a healthy productive citizen, a sheep. If you have a capacity for violence and no empathy for your fellow citizens, then you have defined*

*an aggressive sociopath—a wolf. But what if you have a capacity
for violence, and a deep love for your fellow citizens? What do
you have then? A sheepdog, a warrior, someone who is walking
the hero's path. Someone who can walk into the heart of
darkness, into the universal human phobia, and walk out
unscathed.*

Let me expand on this old U.S. Army soldier's excellent model

of the sheep, wolves, and sheepdogs. We know that the sheep live in

denial; that's what makes them sheep. They do not want to believe

there is evil in the world. They can accept the fact that fires can

happen, which is why they want fire extinguishers, fire sprinklers, fire

alarms, and fire exits throughout their kid's schools.

But many of them are outraged at the idea of putting an armed

police officer in their kid's school. Our children are thousands of times

more likely to be killed or seriously injured by school violence than

fire, but the sheep's only response to the possibility of violence is

denial. The idea of someone coming to kill or harm their child is just

too difficult.

The sheep generally do not like the sheepdog. He looks a lot

like the wolf. He has fangs and the capacity for violence. The

difference, though, is that the sheepdog must not, cannot and will not

ever harm the sheep. Any sheepdog that intentionally harms a little lamb will be punished and removed. The world cannot work any other way, at least not in a representative democracy or a republic such as ours.

Still, the sheepdog disturbs the sheep. He is a constant reminder that there are wolves in the land. They would prefer that he didn't tell them where to go, or give them traffic tickets, or stand at the ready in their airports in camouflage fatigues holding an M16. The sheep would much rather have the sheepdog cash in his fangs, spray paint himself white, and go, "Baa." Until the wolf shows up. Then the entire flock tries desperately to hide behind one lonely sheepdog.

Look at what happened after 9/11, when the wolf pounded hard on the door. Remember how America, more than ever before, felt differently about their law enforcement officers and military personnel? Understand that a sheepdog is a funny critter: He is always sniffing around out the perimeter, checking the breeze, barking at things that go bump in the night, and yearning for a righteous battle. The young ones yearn for a righteous battle, anyway. Old sheepdogs are a little wiser, but, when needed, they move to the sound of the guns right along with the young ones.

Here is how the sheep and the sheepdog think differently: The sheep pretend the wolf will never come, but the sheepdog lives for that day. After the attacks on 9/11, most of the sheep, that is, most citizens in America, said, "Thank God I wasn't on one of those planes." But the sheepdogs said, "Dear God, I wish I could have been on one of those planes. Maybe I could have made a difference."

There is nothing morally superior about the sheepdog, the warrior, but he does have one, and only one, real advantage. He is able to survive and thrive in an environment that destroys 98 percent of the population. Edmund Burke, the eighteenth-century Irish political philosopher, said, "There is no safety for honest men except by believing all possible evil of evil men." That means taking a wait-and-see approach when meeting anyone. It means being prepared to fight or kill anyone who could be evil. It means never being surprised at the devastation an evil person can cause. It means never being outraged at a crime or an Islamic beheading, or any unreal action that a sick, twisted human commits because you do believe all possible evil of evil men. It means suspicion. It means thinking the worst of human beings. It's how you stay alive, and it's a very sad way to live, especially when you've been involved in experiences that prove Burke's quote is true, at least for those who live in the mud with the pigs. You don't walk out

unscathed. Well, I didn't.

Ironically, I would end up doing the very job I railed against in

my letter to my mother. Approximately four years after writing it, I

would be a special agent on the Federal Bureau of Investigation Joint

Terrorism Task Force in Newark, New Jersey, in charge of

investigating all the international terrorism leads affecting New Jersey,

and by proximity, New York City. First, though, I had more to do as a

cop.

For me, 9/11 provided an amazing opportunity for a new

career in law enforcement. Everyone was talking about the new Sky

Security Service. I applied for a position because it sounded

mysterious, elite, and covert—surely a good way to get into espionage

or something like it! Out of two hundred thousand applicants, I was

selected by the Federal Aviation Administration (FAA), based on my

resume of violence, undercover experience, and aggression, to become

one of the first one hundred Federal Air Marshals. I was slated to be in

the second class, which took place in New Mexico, somewhere near

Roswell. The transition was very quick. We were to train for three

months before we took to the skies to do whatever it was we were going to do. At the time, no one really had a plan. We were a half-military, half-law enforcement organization with no real home. The FAA was home to Civil Aviation Security Specialists, otherwise known as Air Marshals. But they really only were a group of about thirty-three former Navy SEALS and Delta Force members sent on specific missions overseas to target particular threats or circumstances. They didn't have law enforcement powers. The FAA, as a regulatory agency, could not, by law, operate as a law enforcement agency. At that time, the Transportation Security Administration hadn't been created. Initially, our orders were under military jurisdiction and we had actual briefings informing us of our "orders of engagement."

But the guys in my class weren't the kind of people who cared much about the name of the agency telling them to do things. All fifty of us were break-glass-in-time-of-emergency people. I can't tell you how honored I was to be included. My class included several Army Rangers; Navy SEALS; a couple of Delta Force guys who don't exist; a couple of Special Forces guys, including a major from 1st Special Forces Group; a bunch of Marine Force Recon guys; and some snipers. The rest of the class was rounded out by cops and troopers from various departments across the country, all with special weapons and tactics or undercover narcotics backgrounds. Being around people

who were that talented at killing things is amazing, and the story

swapping, as we sat and smoked cigars outside at night, was a

highlight of my life.

To put it in perspective, two different movies had been made

about people in my class—*Black Hawk Down* and *Tears of the Sun*.

Being in that environment is intoxicating, addictive, and as removed

from reality as you can imagine. The only things that exist in that

world are bad guys and good guys. Good guys exist to kill the bad guys.

We train to kill the bad guys. Someone in a suit or with bars or stripes

will point out the bad guys and then we will "neutralize" them, with

the minimum amount of force necessary. There are no real

responsibilities—no bills, no housing worries, no food worries. The

days are filled. The nights are for sleeping, cigars, and beer. It's a good

life, if you have a violence switch you can turn on and off. The problem

comes down the road, as it did for me, when one day, the violence

switch wouldn't turn off.

The days in New Mexico were exhausting but stimulating. We

had classroom instruction on explosives, room and building breaching,

kidnapping, espionage, hijacking neutralization, CPR, martial arts, knife fighting, and more. We fired approximately twelve hundred

rounds per day, so many that we had to tape our hands because they

were bleeding. Every week, we needed new guns because we were

heating up the barrels to the point they were warping and cracking.

We ran counterterrorism exercises on various real aircraft. We

became experts at both terrorism and counterterrorism. We learned

about explosives, Improvised Explosive Devices (IEDs), the history of

explosives used in every terrorism incident, and the tactics used in

every terrorism incident. We created better tactics and then counters

to those tactics. We became terrorists to think like terrorists. We

fought each other on planes, in training houses, on mats, and in trains.

We learned surveillance and countersurveillance. We learned "other

stuff, too." We were put under stress tests. We lifted weights, and we

drank a lot of tequila, smoked a lot of cigars, and ate a lot of food

cooked with hot peppers. For the record, we had the best Mexican

cooks ever. Of course, that much testosterone from a large group of

alpha males simmered into some of the nearby towns and bars until

our instructors basically banned us from talking to any women or

starting fights with any men in New Mexico. Eventually, that order

included Lubbock, Texas. So, instead, we drove southwest to El Paso.

My favorite story involves two of our guys eating dinner or breakfast at 3:30 a.m. at the Waffle House near Albuquerque. Now I don't need to tell you what kind of shape you're in if you're at a Waffle House anywhere at 3:30 a.m. One of the guys was a former Marine sniper and the other, a former Navy SEAL. They were about thirty years old and very large humans. Well, an unlucky crackhead walked in and decided to rob the place with a knife about the size of a pair of scissors. In her statement for the police report, the waitress said our guys "started laughing and the robber got confused." After the robber was "helped to unconsciousness," our duo returned to their meals until the police arrived, handcuffed the guy, called an ambulance, and got their names. The next week, they were amusingly showing off the police report.

The environment in which I lived was relaxing in a way I hadn't expected. We weren't asked to fit into society: we were isolated from it. Hell, if we were allowed to go into society, it meant bad things had happened. We could barely fit into what we considered the chaos of a civilized society. We didn't know the social etiquette of the corporate or business world. We didn't know what you could and couldn't say to so-called normal people. We didn't understand that other people didn't threaten each other with violence during disagreements. I didn't understand a confrontation with other strangers could end in any way other than my way. We gave orders, you followed them, or we made you follow them. We were chosen because we were master problem solvers who were good at violence, had a history of undercover abilities, were independent thinkers, and problem solvers. Eventually, I came to realize, each of us had killed at least one person, officially or unofficially, save for an exception or two. For all the military guys in our group, most of us were undercover cops who had essentially spent our lives hunting people, lying to people, trying to kill people, trying to not be killed, and training to do all of the above. We were sheepdogs and some of us probably were wolves that liked being a sheepdog better. But none of us were sheep or comfortable with sheep. Ultimately, we should probably not have been too near the sheep.

Our loyalty to each other shifted to the class, and didn't extend much beyond the class. Eventually, after some physical altercations over who was looking at whom, we were not even allowed to talk to any other classes, nor they to us, even in the dining hall. We were rewarded for fighting hard, shooting well, making quick and violent decisions, and problem solving situations, just as I had on the street.

Although not nearly as good a shooter as several of the other guys, I did win the academic award. (Yeah, Vanderbilt!) My simulations team also was the only one to defeat the instructors in what was supposed to be a losing confrontation. I had little to do with it: two of the Delta Force guys pretty much killed everyone with head shots while advancing into the instructors' line of fire, flanked them, and that was that. It was the damnedest thing I ever saw. The instructors were pissed. You can't hide blue paint all over the front of your face mask and goggles. The trainers were all former SEALS and ex-military from other Special Forces units.

The whole experience was surreal because we weren't given a great deal of information on what we were going to do, where we were going to live, what our job would be, or even whether we'd be law enforcement or some kind of hybrid force. I didn't find out I was moving to New York until one week before I was told to report to New York. I had my wife waiting in Nashville and we were in no financial shape to move. I couldn't even fly home for the four days we had off at Christmas, let alone afford to move. I didn't even have a plan on what I would do when I got to New York. At the time, we didn't know it, but our class was one of an unknown number of small classes – four or five, perhaps - that would be trained the way we were trained, by the

people who trained us, for some special missions. Rather quickly, the

training of Federal Air Marshals moved to Federal Law Enforcement

Training Centers. Congress needed cops on planes, and they wanted

them there quickly. Plus, they'd already had enough of the first group

of us.

The FAA flew me home to Nashville. I unpacked, repacked,

threw a suitcase in my Jeep, and headed north. My Jeep broke down

about five hours outside Nashville. Hilarious. I walked to a

convenience store. Thank God the girl who worked there knew a guy

who fixed cars. I made it to New York the next day. I will never forget

driving over the George Washington Bridge, looking at where the

World Trade Center had stood. I parked on the other side, walked

down to the pier, and smoked a cigar while staring at the Hudson. It

was March, much colder in New York than in Nashville, and I had no

idea what in the hell had happened: What I was doing in New York

City? I could not for the life of me believe my last six months. My mom

always said, "When God decides to move, hold onto your hat."

I spent the next seven days living in my Jeep. The Federal Air

Marshal Service (FAMS), as they later decided to call us, was so brand new that we didn't even have offices. Plus, I couldn't afford a motel at a

hundred bucks per night. I only made a thousand dollars every two

weeks, and that had to pay for my wife to live in Nashville with our

dogs. She was an actress and singer and almost made it. Maybe she still

will. Eventually, though, I was able to stay with the parents of one of

the guys in my class. They are the two dearest people who ever lived

for letting me stay with them. They treated me like family and deserve

the heaven they believe in. Eventually, thanks to some financial help

from my parents and a Federal Housing Administration loan, I was

able to purchase a small house about ninety minutes north of JFK

International Airport in a town near Newburgh, New York. It was a

stupid place to buy a house, but I had no idea what I was doing and

didn't understand the New York/New Jersey area. Suffice it to say that,

before long, I finally was back with my wife and dogs and had a house

in New York. I was very proud of myself.

Chapter 19:

Just Maybe

Spring 2003 Tel Aviv

Once you've lived the inside-out world of espionage, you never shed it. It's a mentality, a double standard of existence.

- John le Carre

The Federal Air Marshal Service is fantastic at two things—

responding quickly to emergencies anywhere in the world and leaking disinformation to mislead the public, another government, or some other entity. With respect to the first thing, a Federal Air Marshal Team has a legal and legitimate reason, under the threat of terrorism or response to an emergency, to enter or exit a foreign country. It can be anywhere in the world as quickly as the next flight takes off. With respect to disinformation, well, that's the interesting part. Maybe you do think the U.S. government spends $800 million a year to fly a bunch of guys from Washington, DC to Los Angeles and back — or maybe, just maybe, some Federal Air Marshals, especially those with backgrounds in undercover work, do other things.

I was assigned rather quickly to an Israeli detail where I spent a great deal of time over the next four years as a team leader. Our missions covered various operations in and around Tel Aviv, most of which were of a protective, or information-gathering, nature. All you really need to know is that, though Israel and the U.S. are friends, they spy the shit out of each other, as every country does to every other country. Because we usually had an overt, official way to enter the country—protecting the flights of United States air carriers, per the Department of Homeland Security—the surveillance and countersurveillance games began immediately after our arrival at Ben

Gurion Airport, just outside Tel Aviv.

The Israelis followed us everywhere, went through our things

every chance they got, and kept both covert and overt surveillance on

us. Next to them, the Russians were the most fun. They liked to use

women to get information on what we were doing, why we were in the

country, who we "really" worked for, and so forth. For some unknown

reason, the Russians were certain we were transferring various pieces

of intelligence in and out of the American Embassy, which we may or

may not have been doing. Everyone accused us of following people

around the world under the guise of Federal Air Marshals protecting

various flights, which we may or may not have been. The Israelis knew

what *they* were doing in the U.S., and given that knowledge, never

quite believed the official line of what *we* FAMs were doing in Israel.

The Russian Embassy is near the Sheraton Tel Aviv Hotel,

where we stayed more than once. The Russians would populate the

bar and lobby area with surveillance people who would pick us up

upon our arrival and stay with us throughout our stay, unless we lost

them. Ultimately, the time I spent in Tel Aviv consisted of a lot of

people following a lot of people around. It was such fun, though we were always worried about kidnappings. Part of our training had

focused on resisting and spotting potential kidnapping scenarios; it

just reinvigorated the idea that you must always be vigilant.

My point is this: everyone is following everyone to see what

they're doing. That goes for cities like Washington, DC, London, New

York, Moscow, lots of them. Living in that world is a lot like turning on

the police radio for the first time. Suddenly, an alternate reality

emerges: things are happening that other people don't see. There's the

world of normal people. Then there's the world of other things. Living

in this other world, an invisible one, like the invisible world of inner

city policing, separated me even further from the everyday reality of

Joe Doctor or Sam Plumber. My everyday world had gone from an

invisible place of suffering to an invisible place of paranoia. Nothing

was normal in this new world, either. I felt like a boat drifting farther

and farther from the shore. One day you look around and try to get

back to shore, only to discover you can't row faster than the current is

pushing you out. It's terrifying.

I kept my focus on the shadow world, the invisible world,

content, at least for a time, to stare straight ahead and wait until a

storm came.

* *

I arrived with my partners in Tel Aviv on April 29, 2003 at approximately 7 a.m. We were there for a reason. Recall early 2002 when everyone knew war was coming to the Middle East. The Middle East Quartet, sometimes called the Diplomatic Quartet or Madrid Quartet or simply the Quartet, is a foursome of nations and international and supranational entities involved in mediating the peace process in the Israeli-Palestinian conflict. The Quartet comprises the United Nations, the United States, the European Union (EU), and Russia. The group was established in 2002, as a result of the escalating conflict in the Middle East. Recall the United States ramping up for war with Iraq and Afghanistan, and the escalating violence between Israel and Palestine. On October 25, 2001, Quartet representatives met Palestinian leader Yasser Arafat and loudly expressed support for his policy of a cease-fire and reform in the Palestinian Authority. Of course, the cease-fire didn't last. About a month later, eleven Israeli civilians, nine of them teenagers, were killed and 188 injured in a Hamas suicide bombing attack. A month after that, the al-Aqsa Martyrs' Brigades, a coalition of Palestinian armed groups in the West Bank, committed the Bat Mitzvah massacre, a January 17, 2002 terrorist attack in Hadera, Israel in which six people were killed and

33 were wounded at a Bat Mitzvah celebration. So, the Palestinians

and Israelis got back at it soon after.

During the Israeli incursions into Palestinian areas in April

2002, the Quartet met in Madrid and again called for implementation

of cease-fire agreements. The violence escalated and continued in

2002, and finally, in March 2003, President Arafat nominated

Mahmoud Abbas for the post of the first prime minister. On April 29,

2003, the day we arrived, the Palestinian Parliament approved the

appointment. But a struggle for power between Abbas and Arafat, as

well as members of the old Palestinian Authority and Hamas, made the

Palestinian Parliament's decision unpopular with some Palestinians.

On April 28, 2003, a day before our arrival, President Bush made a

very important speech in Dearborn, Michigan, in which he discussed

the future of Iraq and the upcoming end of Operation Iraqi Freedom. In

a place marred by fighting for thousands of years, April 29 and April

30 were shaping up to be important dates, and everyone knows how

dangerous those can be in Israel.

We'd been working off of general intelligence that a terrorist

attack could occur near the American Embassy in Tel Aviv in the very near future. Given all the above information, anyone with an ounce of

understanding of the Israeli/Palestine conflict could see the danger

coming. Upon our arrival, we immediately began the fun and

somewhat irritating game of "who's following whom," as I liked to call

it. Of course, the Russians, with their embassy so very close to ours,

were always involved. Israel, however, did something unusual in its

dealings with us. They ran us through the ringer upon our arrival and

then left us alone —except for the car which followed us and the

omnipresent guy and girl, acting like a couple, who checked into the

hotel with us.

You really never know who or how many people are tailing you

without taking severe and complicated countersurveillance measures,

so if you don't have the time to make sure you are truly alone, you just

assume everything you do is being watched. You can catch some with

countersurveillance maneuvers, which we always employed. But we

weren't in-country in the same way as more traditional diplomats. So

we didn't have the time to establish routines and schedules or take

long drives. When we were in-country for extended periods of time,

we would employ such measures, but this time we were here because

worries existed that the American Embassy could be a target. The

Israelis who usually paralleled us were obviously busy, which was

definitely an indication that they were worried about other, more

dangerous, things.

We checked into our hotel and canvassed the area. We checked

the lobbies and bars of the nearby hotels, talked with the security

guards, walked around the American Embassy, and surveilled the

immediate area for any type of suspicious behavior. The Isrotel has an

outdoor pool on its top—twenty-eighth— floor with a wonderful view

of the city and so was a good place to scope things out with binoculars

and get a feel for how the city, like a living organism, was moving that

day. By 11 p.m., we were out of ideas and hadn't seen anything that

could be deemed suspicious. We'd talked to every local in the area

with an outdoor food or beach stand and anyone who would be in a

position to notice suspicious people out of place in their area.

The American Embassy is one street past the beach and Retsif

Herbert Samuel Street, which runs along the beach. The embassy is on

Ha-Yarkon Street, which is one street closer to the beach than Ben

Yahuda Street—a very popular local gathering area full of bars,

nightclubs, and restaurants that dead ends into Allenby Street to the

south. As you move away from the beach, across Retsif Herbert Samuel

Street, the elevation increases dramatically — maybe 20 feet or more

— to Ha-Yarkon Street and the embassy.

At 11:30 p.m. we went to a favorite hangout called Mike's

Place, a bar and cafe situated behind the American Embassy, between

Retsif Herbert Samuel and Ha-Yarkon streets. It always has great food,

live sports —including good soccer games, my favorite —and a pool

table we liked to use. We'd sit and shoot pool while paying special

attention to the bartender. She was a beauty. She said her name was

Sarah and one of us was always trying to get her to go to dinner. There

was a bell above the bar that Sarah would ring when she got a good tip

— an obnoxious cowbell. We'd always tip her nicely to get her to ring

the shit out of the bell but mostly to get her attention. She was five foot

seven with black hair streaked with sun. Sarah loved the ocean and

adored that she could always see it while at work. She wore ripped

jeans shorts, sandals, and a tee shirt, rolled tight. She was always

hanging and rehanging a stupid long string of Guinness cardboard beer

mugs, which folded out like paper dolls, from the ceiling at the front of

the bar to the ceiling near the back of the bar. It always fell down. OK,

maybe it was occasionally pulled down by I don't know who. I would

tease her about the cardboard mugs all the time.

That night, I walked over and she yelled at me for pretending to yank them down. I ordered a coffee and she shot me a look. She suspected who we were and every time any of us ordered a coffee or tea instead of a Guinness or Maccabee, she poked fun.

"Oh, really?" she'd say. I remember looking at the beach and the wide boardwalk across the street that night, watching the people walk by. Like Spain, Israel is a country that stays up late, even on a Tuesday. At 12 a.m., we left Mike's Place and walked up the block again. We went to the American Embassy, down to the beach, across Restif Herbert Samuel Street, and then up to Mike's Place. There's a rule that's important to follow in Israel: when you sit in a bar or cafe without multiple security guards outside, you sit in the back of the place. Never sit in the front.

At 12:45 a.m. on April 30, the song "Ain't No Sunshine," by Bill Withers, was playing. The place was fairly crowded. We were in the back. I was looking at one of the bartenders, who was very pretty, and talking to Kyle about leaving and going to Allenby Street to see if Joey's, an American bar, still had security around it. The bartender's face flashed a panicked look, just like in the movies when someone's eyes get big and the camera pans to whatever they're seeing. It's never good. There was a yell, then another, and then a boom like a huge,

thunderous gunshot. I'd been to bomb school and had witnessed tons

of explosions, but this one was far closer than I'd ever heard. In that

instant, it was as if a two-second tornado struck. Everything went

flying: glasses, beer bottles, and mirrors shattered, spraying glass

everywhere. I found myself in the back corner, on the ground, with a

chair on me. My brain screamed, *Secondary bomber!* There's always a

secondary bomber. I looked for a way out, but there wasn't one. People

were screaming and lifting themselves over tables and chairs as they

tried to get by the picnic tables, pool table, and other bodies to go

outside. Blood was sprayed over the floor. The entire white frame of

the outside seating area had fallen inside. The security guard who'd

been out front was wounded.

As we got out, I ran across the street, looking frantically for the

secondary bomber. *If I could find him*, I thought, *I might be able to help

in some way*. But amid the chaos there was no way to see anyone

looking suspicious. We ran to the beach. When sirens sounded, I knew

we had to get out of there. I couldn't believe the devastation I saw.

The suicide bomber who had targeted Mike's Place blew

himself up at the entrance. That security guard, who, I would later

learn, was named Avi Tabib, had saved us. He'd managed to block the
suicide bomber, preventing him from entering the bar and causing
further fatalities. Nevertheless, the force of the blast killed three
people and injured more than fifty.

Later, we also would learn that immediately after the first
attack, another suicide bomber, who was carrying a concealed
explosive belt, was supposed to carry out another attack. I don't know
if it was supposed to also be at Mike's Place. I guess we'll never know.
The second bomber, whose device failed to detonate, fled to the David
InterContinental Hotel, right down the road. He ended up fighting
with a security guard and then fled from that hotel. He probably was
killed by his own people insofar as he floated dead onto the beach
about two weeks later. The two bombers were members of the radical
Islamic Al-Muhajiroun, a British member-group of al Qaeda.

I remember making the standard calls and then calling my
mom and dad to tell them we were OK and not really involved. I
snapped two pictures as the medical personnel and police arrived. I
wanted to remember this failure. I know we were hunting for a needle
in a haystack, but we had just missed that needle. If we'd been outside
instead of inside, we could have saved even more people.

Intellectually, I know it was luck we'd even guessed right enough to be close to Mike's Place and not some other bar or cafe. But if we'd stayed outside a bit longer, or if we'd walked a different route past the embassy, it all could have been different. Instead, there were bodies, blood, and lots of injured people. By the way, Sarah lived, and, of all things, that damn string of cardboard Guinness beer mugs stayed put. I took a picture of that, too. I had a scraped knee that bled through my jeans, just as if I'd fallen off my bike twenty years earlier.

That moment in the explosion, when I waited to see if I'd die in the blast wave, was just a second. The weird thing is that the blast wave will hit you before the sound wave . So if you hear the explosion, you may be alive. It all happens in a second and a second lasts three eye blinks. Blink three times. Boom.

Chapter 20:

Clarence Gets His

Wings

You drown not by falling into a river, but by staying submerged in it.

— Paulo Coelho

September 2005, New Orleans

I was one of two air marshals from the Newark, New Jersey

Field Office to respond to Hurricane Katrina. First, I was sent to Atlanta

to gather more FAM teams. From there, we all flew into the sewer and

pool that was New Orleans. We were deputized Louisiana State Police

and we were headquartered in what was once the Louis Armstrong

New Orleans International Airport, but was then a giant mess of Red

Cross stations, medical stations, a makeshift hospital, a morgue, and

the new jail. When the door to our aircraft opened, FAM medics were

waiting to give us various injections for God knows what. We just went

down the line—left arm, right arm, left arm, right arm. We got four or

five shots, and I probably have an alien growing inside of me now. I'm

fine with being used as an alien stud as long as there's a potential

chance whatever they put into my system could result in a superpower

or two. Centers for Disease Control and Prevention Director Dr. Julie

Gerberding later announced that sewage-related bacteria in the New

Orleans floodwaters were at ten times the maximum allowable level

and warned those still in the city not to touch the water. Yuck. Anyway,

from there I put down my stuff on a cot alongside another fifty or more

cots, turned in all directions. Elsewhere in the terminal, the National

Guard had its cots. It was time to go to work.

On Thursday, September 1, New Orleans Mayor Ray Nagin had

this to say about the state of the crime in the city in an interview with

WWL, a local radio station: "Drugs flowed in and out of New Orleans

and the surrounding metropolitan area so freely it was scary to me,

and that's why we were having the escalation in murders. People don't

want to talk about this, but I'm going to talk about it. You have drug

addicts that are now walking around this city looking for a fix, and

that's the reason why they were breaking in hospitals and drugstores.

They're looking for something to take the edge off of their

'withdrawal,' if you will. And right now, they don't have anything to

take the edge off. And they've probably found guns. So what you're

seeing is drug-starving crazy addicts, drug addicts, that are wreaking

havoc. And we don't have the manpower to adequately deal with it. We

can only target certain sections of the city and form a perimeter

around them and hope to God that we're not overrun."

Soon afterward, a fleet of military helicopters and buses with

military and law enforcement escorts somewhat succeeded in

emptying the darkened hospitals throughout the city's flooded zones.

My new home—the departures concourse of the airport—had become

the newest and most chaotic hospital in the New Orleans area. By

Friday afternoon, a ton of commercial jets were arriving. By evening, all the patients from the flooded zones had been moved out, though

hundreds of medical personnel and frightened city residents who had

sought shelter in hospitals from rising water were still hoping

someone would come get them, too. Left behind also were an unknown

number of people dead in flooded morgues.

The airport had become triage center, morgue, and one of the

bases of operations for helicopters searching for people and bodies as

well as the commercial aircraft we were using to evacuate the dead,

dying, and others who were soon to be relocated. As I walked through

the terminal, on my way to the helicopter I was assigned to join, I took

in dramas all around me. Some of those who'd been rescued were

accepting water from the National Guard while others were having

spasms on stretchers. Some people were dying; others already were

dead. When I walked by a woman with brown eyes and salt-and-

pepper hair, sitting in a wheelchair, I closed her eyes and covered her

with a blue Delta Air Lines blanket. Mentally deranged people

wandered the triage area. Many were urinating and defecating on the

floor, while others were babbling quietly, shaking violently, or chewing

on their lower lips. *The mentally ill,* I thought, *always the forgotten*

souls. The smells of death, urine, and shit were overpowering. I made my way out of the terminal and onto the tarmac. FAMs were driving

baggage carts from the helicopters to the terminal, some with recently

dead people, carefully laid out and covered.

Giant white tents erected by the Red Cross housed a hundred

picnic tables with various FAM and National Guard personnel, too

exhausted to continue without a recharge—a quick bite to eat, or a nap

in the shade. I was to find out there were no shifts and no real orders.

Everyone worked incessantly doing whatever needed to be done until

they couldn't lift their eyelids anymore. Then they grabbed an hour of

sleep and did some more. I jumped into the nearest helicopter and

took off with a FAM team.

New Orleans was flooded, all right. Flying around gave me a

jaw-dropping view of just how bad the devastation was. New Orleans

looked empty and wet. Smoke was rising from various places and

when you looked at streets, all you saw were rooftops and rivers.

These are just a few of the problems we faced: We had to

evacuate the remaining hospital patients. City residents who'd gone to

the hospitals also were waiting to be evacuated. It was just dawning on

everyone that the nursing homes, which also needed to be evacuated, could easily have been turned into floating morgues. Murders were

occurring. A great number of illegal immigrants were dead and

unidentifiable.

I spent the majority of the days at various hospitals , including

Memorial Medical Center, helping to evacuate patients and other

citizens, and the Armstrong airport, where we were beginning to fly

rescue and relocation flights. The hospitals were a mess. Generators

had shut off in some areas, and water and chaos surrounded us. The

heat was making everything even more horrible as doctors and nurses

struggled to get patients anywhere safe and dry. The smells of sewage,

hot garbage, sickness, and death permeated the air. Since the lower

areas of the hospitals were flooded, we helped get patients into the

parking garages or other areas where they could be taken by truck or

helicopter to the airport or anywhere else. Bodies, bloated and lifeless,

floated down some streets. The corpse of one overweight man wearing

dark pants and a green shirt was wrapped around a stop sign, as if

some macabre god had placed him there. How quickly the First World

had become the Third World. I didn't think or feel very much. I just

worked, stunned at what had happened to New Orleans.

I helped lift one old man off a hospital bed and onto a stretcher.

We were going to carry him to the evacuation area near the parking
garage. He had a hold of my wrist, near my gloves, and gripped me like
he was hanging from the top of a cliff. He knew the slightest breeze
could take him from this world. The old man was sick, very sick. I
asked him his name, and, after some moments, he was able to wheeze
a response.

"Clarence Jaspers," he said. Clarence was made to look even
frailer than he was by the debris, waters, moans, and sounds all
around us. They were sounds that weren't supposed to be at a
hospital. You always picture yourself dying in a hospital, hopefully
with your children or grandchildren gathered around you. Perhaps
there will be some flowers brightly coloring a shelf near the window,
you think, and some of those awkward corner chairs all hospital rooms
have for whatever family members are assigned to the vigil. A
comforting nurse will be there, you think, to firmly but gently and, in a
motherly way, make sure you're resting comfortably and taking your
medicine. She'll make sure you're not too thirsty.

Years later in Englewood Hospital in New Jersey, I would sit in
one of those awkward chairs, my wife in the one next to me, as we sat
vigil for Jeff, her first husband and her son's father. We were there for

Jeff's last moments, courtesy of pancreatic cancer. He slipped in and

out of pain and morphine, suspended between worlds but clearly done

with this one. Jeff woke up and hazily asked me to help him to the

bathroom. As I picked him up in my arms, as if he were a small child, I

felt his last breath leave his body. I placed him, gently as I could, back

into his hospital bed, kissed him on the forehead, and called in the

doctor. I was sad for Jeff and even sadder for my wife's son, Justin, who

had just lost his father. But Jeff's death was a good death, if only in the

sense that he passed while surrounded by people who radiated love

for him. As the husband of his son's mother, I certainly was an odd

person to be involved in such an intimate situation. But he and I

always had a great relationship and we did what we could for him. At

that point, I'd seen death over and over again, so I think I was a good

person to be there, by his side. My wife grieved all the things Jeff

wouldn't be around to see for their son — graduating from college,

falling in love, building a life, perhaps having kids. True, all those

potential experiences were being extinguished, second by second. Still,

Jeff's death was a good one. He was loved, and we made sure he knew

it. That's about the best comfort someone can have.

Clarence didn't have even one beloved person by his deathbed.

He was jaundiced and it was clear his kidneys were failing, or had failed. I didn't know. But Clarence, his frail hand locked on my wrist with such clear determination and yet with such weakness, looked up at me, searching, I think, for recognition of someone—some family member or friend. The soldier from the National Guard and I halted the stretcher and I motioned for him to help me put it down on the ground. We did so gently, lest the jarring cause his fragile soul to leave quicker than it was supposed to leave. The young soldier and I held Clarence's frail hands.

"Clarence, you leave this world loved and with friends," I told him. "We will never forget you and you will live on in our hearts. Close your eyes, if you need to." That was a good enough ending for Clarence, and under the circumstances, the best we could give him. Clarence did close his eyes. We picked up the stretcher and carried it toward the helicopter. It wasn't until I felt his small, thin hand fall from my wrist that I knew he was gone. I don't know if Clarence was a good man or not, and I'm not sure that question really matters in the last moment any of us have on earth. We all face death alone, truly. But I like to think that Clarence knew we would remember him, and I will. That was my promise. When I watched Jeff die, I remembered Clarence.

That day turned into night and then into another day. The landscape was all the same—flooded, dirty, disgusting. Sometimes, while flying, we heard gunshots and tried to locate their origin, but it often was too difficult. The animals remained the animals; now they had a proper environment for their behavior. We could look down into higher parking garages and structures and see small bands of scum taking advantage of the plight of the city. We were on rescue missions, so we didn't stop to kill them. Maybe we should have.

We were finally able to start ferrying the sick, elderly, and other survivors out of the airport and to Houston, then other places. As the sick died or left, the airport population changed to drug addicts going through withdrawal; street whores, also going through crack and meth withdrawal; and criminals who knew it was time to hitch a ride out of New Orleans. Farm animals act better than these people did. They were annoying and somewhat aggressive. Any place became an acceptable place to piss or shit, which made for some conflict with our code, which was not to let people piss or shit wherever they wanted. A lot of them had found guns and knives in the streets, knew they weren't supposed to have them, and would just set them down and walk away. Eventually, where they entered the airport, we put out a box where they could place their guns and knives. We filled up those boxes and then some. Our duties turned back into police duties as we managed the evacuation of these lovely residents. Finally, we ferried a group to Illinois on a commercial jet. From there, I was shuttled back to Newark, and that, my friends, was that.

Except that it wasn't. It should have been. But I couldn't shake some real outrage. Bringing relief to New Orleans shouldn't have happened the way it did, and that made me very angry with the U.S. government. The whole process was a betrayal of what our country is supposed to do for its people. I saw a link between working in the ghettos and working in New Orleans. In both places, all the "good" people ignored the real problems because those problems don't really affect them in their day-to-day lives. But then something happens to break through the circled wagons. In this case, a flood broke through and they called us in to clean it up. I can't put my finger on what's wrong with us. I can still hear the sound my boots made slushing on the thin, blue, fecal- and urine-stained carpet in the airport. I can still see outside the window to where Red Cross tents covered such a large part of the tarmac. We just don't do a good job of prevention. We know we can call in people who will keep responding, keep fixing, keep carrying on.

There was a long list of reasons why the government failure was so catastrophic. When all was said and done, though, it seems the government just didn't give a shit and was unprepared. Oversimplification? You bet. So what? My shoulders felt very heavy from all the new memories and scenes of death and sadness. I felt very guilty for even thinking a sad thought because of all the people who had lost so much. So I took the feelings and shoved them down, with all the other ones.

They kept coming back, though. They surfaced in nightmares and memories. For me, Katrina was the straw that broke the camel's back, as the saying goes. It added just enough weight to threaten to pull me under the water of despair. Remember when I told you that you have to shut out everything, or one thing can get in. You can't let that one thing get inside you. A single drop of water will start the dam breaking. I could almost sense my imminent sinking.

Chapter 21:

Gilligan's Best

Friend,

The Skipper

Summer has come and passed
The innocent can never last

— Green Day,"Wake Me Up When September

Ends"

August 2005, Nashville

I don't know what happened because I wasn't there. Randy chased a guy into an apartment in the John Henry Hale projects. Big Randy wasn't ever going to get you in the sprint, but he was going to corner you and then come in for the tackle. The apartments were almost all the same: When you walk in, the kitchen is to the right. Directly ahead is the staircase. At the top of the stairs is the bathroom. To the right is a short hallway, located over the kitchen, with a bedroom on either side of the hall. Randy would have entered the apartment, glanced into the kitchen to see if the back door was ajar, and then slowly headed up the stairs, his back to the wall, slightly canted toward the bedrooms to the right. The shower curtain always posed a tactical problem. There also wasn't a good way to see behind the bathroom door when it was half closed. Usually, though, only people in Hitchcock movies hide behind the shower curtain. Nevertheless, Randy would have ripped it aside with his left hand while holding his gun in his right, with his back against the bathroom mirror, still canted toward the bedrooms. The bathroom clear, he would have exited and probably gone to the bedroom on the right side of the hall. The window was opposite the door. The real problem was the long closet, also opposite the window, on the same side wall as the door. The closet doors, though paper thin, were made of wood, so you couldn't see inside the closet. There was no good way to search the closet. To slide it open, you had to expose yourself. Randy never got that far. They told me the shots blazed through the slightly ajar sliding door, just as he approached the closet.

Randy was hit three times, one shot in the pelvis dropping him to the ground. He managed to fire off two magazines into the closet, still uncertain from which of the long sliding doors the shots were coming. Those twenty rounds or so were enough to hit the unseen suspect, wounding him, and ending the gunfire.

Randy was taken by ambulance to Vanderbilt University Medical Center and into surgery, where he was saved. I'll never forget receiving the call from a Nashville sergeant who was friends with Randy and me for a long time. I wanted to scream. My anger exploded. Randy was the last person who should be lying in a pool of his own blood in the ghetto. Randy was going to be a doctor, like his dad, but he just loved the police job. He was always happy, always laughing, always giving you his big hugs. He'd just gotten married, too, and had an eight-year-old stepdaughter. I'd encouraged him to join my old unit,

West FLEX, because the projects had been "such fun," and now he was

in the hospital. I was on the next flight to Nashville.

I hugged Randy and he opened his eyes a little bit — the

Skipper and his "Little Buddy." I held in my tears until he fell back

asleep, a couple of seconds later. Then I went to the lobby and sobbed.

If I was still in Nashville, still on that unit, Randy wouldn't have been

shot. I knew that then and I know that now. Deep down, I knew the job

had broken me and that I was ruined inside. I wept because I knew

Randy would be ruined now, too. I knew the black hole of rage had

infected him, and I knew the blackness never went away. I blamed

myself. I never should have left. I was trying to make a new life

somewhere, having just begun dating my soon-to-be second wife. All

those stupid dreams of being a hero. All the stupid quixotic ideals. I'd

just been selected as the FBI's Newark Joint Terrorism Task Force

representative from the Federal Air Marshal Service. I was going to

work to stop terrorism in this country? For whom? Anonymous

people? In the meantime, my best friend was shot and possibly dying

and I could have prevented that if I'd just stayed his partner on that

gangs/drugs unit. I never would have left him alone to clear that

apartment.

That day, I was realizing something clearly and powerfully: There was no way to win this game. There were only ways to lose more. There was nothing I could do to save friends unless I was by their side. Despair flooded me—gut-wrenching despair. There was no hope. Nothing in this world was worth Randy, who, day after day, worked to help those in need. So that was it for me. After that, I stopped making friends. There was no friend better than Randy and, if I couldn't save him, I was a worthless friend.

I haven't had a male friend since Randy. As I write this, it's been almost fifteen years. I don't make an effort to connect with men. I'm not even comfortable thinking of males as friends. I'm sure some shrink reading this can explain that or at least give a good theory or tie up some loose ends. Funny thing is, I never talked to Randy after he recovered. It was too painful. After some horrific event or another, people used to ask Randy how I was doing. Randy told me he'd always answer those people, "He'll be alright."

Isn't that a funny answer? "Alright" means alive and moving forward in some manner, but not necessarily much more. As for "will be," that's future tense. I never really was alright after that, and I knew Randy wouldn't be alright, either. I couldn't bear to lose the Randy who was always happy, always kind; the Randy who truly believed in helping people because they were worthy of help; the Randy who loved the story about saving me in the fight with the armed guy. That Randy, I realized, would disappear into the black, raging ball of hatred. Out would come Randy Who Hated with all his heart and soul. I couldn't talk to that Randy. I already had enough of that inside me. I guess if you ask me how I think Randy's doing, I'd say, "I hope he will be alright." Future tense.

Around the time of Randy's shooting, my terrorism task force squad was assigned to investigate and triage every international terrorism threat to New Jersey. Since the state is across the Hudson River from New York City, there was a lot of work. I worked with amazing and extremely accomplished investigators from the FBI, CIA, Secret Service, U.S. Defense Department, Newark Police Department, NYPD, and other agencies and departments. It was an honor to serve the country with them. We handled some cases that were very public and mitigated dangerous situations the public will never know about. During my time with the FBI, I was involved in the arrest and prosecution of three notable cases, and our squad was even involved in the Fort Dix Six. The FBI Joint Terrorism Task Force arrested six

Muslim men from New Jersey and Philadelphia on May 8, 2007 and

charged them with planning to attack the fort with automatic

weapons, and possibly grenades, in an attempt to kill as many soldiers

as they could. In October 2008, the six were prosecuted in federal

court. On December 22, 2008, five were found guilty of conspiracy to

commit murder, four received life sentences, and one received a thirty-

three-year prison term. The remaining member was sentenced to five

years in prison for weapons offenses.

I also was involved in the arrest and prosecution of an

individual who threatened to put ten bombs on ten Coach USA buses

as they drove through the Lincoln Tunnel, and in the case of Akhtar

Hussain Muawia, a favored assassin with Sipah-e-Sahaba Pakistan

(SSP), a sectarian group that has been blamed for the massacres of

Pakistani civilians as it pushed a pro-Sunni, anti-American agenda. He

was to be deported to Pakistan and sentenced to the death penalty. Let

me just say there's a lot I'd like to say about these five years, but I can't.

But the essence of the story—my story—isn't about

investigations or mitigated terrorism events. It's about the brewing

cauldron of inaction that I couldn't emotionally handle. For many

years, I'd run at red hot temperatures into more and more danger. I'd run as fast as I could to escape the memories, black depression, and

brutal pain. Suddenly, I was running no more. I wasn't kicking down

doors and fighting. I wasn't in a battle; I was in an office. I was safe.

That's when the ultimate realization hit me: I wasn't going to die on

the job. I was going to live. There would be no hero's memorial. I had

betrayed myself: I wasn't risking my life to save someone or for some

grand idea. I was putting on a suit and studying documents. My brain

reeled, bucked, and spit. I had convinced myself that my only value

would be to give my life. The shame crushed me so completely, it's

difficult to describe. I felt as if I'd betrayed every single cop who gave

his or her life in the line of duty. I still feel that betrayal today, too.

According to the National Law Enforcement Officers Memorial

Fund, on average, one officer is killed somewhere in the country every

fifty-eight hours. I'd read their stories on the Officer Down Memorial

Page; I'd read entries by their wives, mothers, daughters, and sons, and

I had left messages and poems to their surviving families and to the

dead themselves. I always wrote to tell them that their lives were not

given in vain and that we would not forget them.

But I now was betraying all they'd lived for, all they'd died for,

and all their memories stood for. The weight of it pressed me from the head down. For five years, from 2005 to Summer 2009, I tried

everything to lift the weight, to remove the burden, but it would not

budge. Not an inch. So I decided to drink until someone came and got

me. It wasn't a conscious decision. It was the last, desperate play of

someone who knew he had only one desperate play left. It was my last

cry for help.

Chapter 22:

Shattered Me

"The mind is its own place, and in itself can make a heaven of hell, a hell of heaven..."

— John Milton, *Paradise Lost*

August 2009, New Jersey

I don't remember when I started drinking to pass out at night, but I remember why: I wanted to stop the adrenaline and slow down my hypervigilance and the damn night terrors. Though I was utterly exhausted all the time, I couldn't sleep. If I didn't slow down my brain,

it wouldn't fall sleep. Not after nights of being in fights and car chases.

If I didn't pass out at night, I'd wake up yelling and covered in sweat,

and night terrors were no fun. So I just made sure to down some vodka

or a bottle of wine before bed. One day, for no single reason I can put

my finger on, all the compartments and walls, castles and ramparts I'd

built in my mind for years against all the demons, monsters, and

memories just collapsed. When my defenses fell, a vile emotional army

attacked my soul with a vengeance that had been pent up longer than a

decade. You could say my brain went to war with me, bombarding me

with flashbacks of all the violence I'd committed, swirling up guilt and

rage, firing off adrenaline and other chemicals, and spinning a swirling

vortex of black depression and hatred. I guess my brain had decided

that it already hurt enough and would, once and for all, end the pain.

When I responded with a salvo of vodka, Fort Sumter quickly enlarged

into a full-blown civil war.

I still saw what I could have become—a surgeon, a lawyer, an

astronomer, a senator, a man admired, a man who had done good

deeds and created things of value. Then my brain held up my small

crying, black, shriveled soul, and screamed, *What did you do? For what?*

We could have done so much. It showed me what I had destroyed of that brown-haired boy who'd been taught not to hit, not to take things that don't belong to him, not to swear, and to always share. I wept as my brain kept screaming at me with such fury that I'd stare in the mirror and scream at myself. I'd drink a full bottle of vodka in front of the mirror and stare, with hatred, at the reflection. I'd stare until I couldn't see. Still, I couldn't stop the adrenaline from flowing. I couldn't close my eyes and block out the pain. The betrayal I felt was too great.

My wife found me in my black Dodge truck in the back of the cab, weeping.

"I want to die," I told her. But even in that, I had failed. I had held my gun, daring myself to pull the trigger, unsure who, exactly, would be killed or whether the pain would stop even after I did it. My brain screamed on, *You goddamned fucking coward*! It flashed images—me being held with a gun in my mouth while working undercover narcotics, and dead body after dead body. I tried to block the images with the booze wall, but it was like the wall wasn't even there. *You are broken!*

"I am!" I wailed. But my brain drowned me out in a voice that sounded as if all the glass in the world had shattered at once: *Die!* But whatever was left of that little boy just wouldn't pull the trigger. So I wept, feeling ashamed and unforgivable, feeling I'd let down every fallen hero, my family, my wife, my stepson, my stepdaughter, all I could have been but would never be. Despair is a word that's rarely used because it's difficult to adequately define. But when you feel irredeemable, it's despair that rips you apart and leaves you for dead — sometimes inside, sometimes outside, sometimes both.

* *

Insofar as I was armed, I was technically a danger to myself and others and ended up in a mental hospital. The ambulance took me to a place in Southern New Jersey and checked me in for post-traumatic stress disorder. Upon arrival, the staff tried to take my shoelaces and belt. I gave them my belt, but I refused to give them my shoelaces. I guess I was holding onto the last remnant of control I had over the situation. I don't know how many orderlies it would have taken to get my shoelaces off my shoes, but it quickly became apparent how many they were going to use. So I stood there, squared off to all of them, and did the only thing I could rationally do: surrender. I didn't surrender, mind you, but my shoelaces did. After their sneaky little injection, surrender was moot. I woke up that evening in my institutional bed. I met a lot of good, messed-up people in there. I hope they all made it. As for me, I was realizing my career was over. I was another casualty of simply being in law enforcement.

I would lie on my bed, staring at the off-white ceiling and thinking about my wife, my fourteen-year-old stepdaughter, and my stepson, who was in college at the time. My wife and I celebrated our first anniversary with me in the mental facility. We sat outside on a picnic table and she got to see my new hairdo. I had buzzed off most of my hair in some weird cathartic attempt. I was still following some movie script, maybe. Anyway, she hated it. As we sat outside, she gave me my birthday present—an empty journal with a brown leather cover. She told me to write all the reasons I had for coming back to the world on its pages. She told me to write a letter to my stepdaughter, Jordan, too. She wanted me to come back to her as the man she married. But I felt that man was now forever broken.

I knew I was an abject failure as a husband, stepfather, cop, son, brother, and person. Memories were crushing my mind. A black internal rage was suffocating me. I needed to find my way out of the pain. I played the piano. I had done that at Vanderbilt to make money in college. The music calmed me. I played slow, sad notes until the sadness filled the small room and stung my eyes. I played angry notes until the wolf howled at the deep, low, tones. I played high, ethereal notes, delicately, as if they were coming from a music box. In my mind, I watched a music box dancer twirl and twirl: I played until she stopped. Only then, ever so softly, would I end. But I played a great deal and thought a great deal, the notes goading me in their emotional directions.

One day I was sitting on my piano bench playing sadness and looking at the window. A spider walked up the window, on the outside. It began to spin a web. I had never seen a spider spin a web before. It began at one top corner of the window, attached the web there and dropped to the bottom corner. She then walked to the other bottom corner, and finally, returned to the top, spinning all the way. She spun for over an hour, around and around, until she had a beautiful web, almost perfectly symmetrical. When it was complete, she rested and waited for lunch to come to her web. That spider made something more beautiful in an hour than I ever could in a lifetime. I vowed to myself in the moment to carry spiders outside rather than kill them. I didn't feel worthy to kill them. I shouldn't—not I who had created

nothing as beautiful, who felt ruined forever. After I was medically

retired out of law enforcement, I had no plan, no existence. I would

have no need for everything I was, everything I trained for, every skill I

had earned the hard way. In return, society would have no need of me.

So I sat, staring out the window, past the spider web. I was

thirty-five and had only tales of destruction. I would have to choose to

live in some other way. Doing what? I could not even lift my eyelids

because the weight of the shame of my hospitalization was too great.

What was hospitalization but the ultimate failure, a failure of living? If

wind or rain blew away the spider's web, she could create another, just

as beautiful. The storms had knocked me down, but I was not a

creator. I had never created anything. I had just taken life away, I was

always involved in death.

It was 9 a.m. on Tuesday when I was to leave the hospital and I

had a decision to make: live or die. I closed my eyes and let the swirl of

hate, rage, shame, and darkness sweep over me, as it did with such

ease. I let the wolf come and snarl and growl. I felt his teeth rip into the

little boy, shattering and destroying him, as the wolf had done so many

times before. I saw Anthony Franklin on Death Row. I saw the pedophile I had left to rape his son. I saw the men I'd shot, the men I'd

beaten. I saw Mike and Randy and DJ. I saw the corpses in New Orleans

and the body parts in Tel Aviv. I saw each monster come for me and rip

into me. I turned inward and dove deeper and deeper into the

blackness, knowing I was lost and that this would be my last chance,

my last search, my last fight. I dove into the abyss, slamming into the

monsters, one by one, fighting each one again. Only this time I threw

images back into them. I fired at them all the love my mother had for

her little boy. I struck at them, time and again, with the perseverance

my father had taught the eight-year-old Ryan who'd broken his finger

in a soccer game. I drowned them with the tears my sister cried for the

loss of her hero, her brother who'd never given up on anything but was

giving up now. I accepted the love of my wife and stepdaughter and let

it disintegrate the shame that had choked the air from my lungs and

left me with no words.

I fought and I fought, and when the boy reached the bottom of

the abyss, the end of himself, he saw nothing but blackness and

despair. *I am not dead*, he said. *Please fight for me!* Together, for the

first time, the wolf and the boy pushed back the hatred, the anger, the

rage, the monsters. From the darkness came a light, small and fragile, but with the strength of a million stars. It had never gone out, even

when the boy could not see it and the wolf could not sense it.

The battle for my life was won by the inextinguishable light of

love. I had to believe in something so I believed others would forgive

me. I believed they loved me. With only that light to shine, I walked out

of the mental hospital, ready to begin again.

Epilogue

If you're going through hell, keep going.

—Winston Churchill

March 2014, New Jersey

Turns out, I was right to believe. I love my life now. The boy inside me is sensitive, kind, caring, and silly. But the wolf is quick to temper, black with hate and rage, and loves chaos. It's important that my life is calm and simple, and I work to keep it that way. I study a great deal. I love history, science, and technology. I always loved to learn. So I pursue those interests.

I have some vague anger and self-hatred for not having pursued some grander or more successful and less mentally damaging direction. It's taken me some time to figure out exactly what's left of me or for me, what I should do, or where I should go. Post-traumatic stress has polarized me into two people—a wolf and a boy. They still fight, every day. I have a powerful rage inside me that sits and waits for a chance to be a hero; it pulls on me, reminding me this chapter of my life is not one from which I can quietly walk away. The wolf is waiting for a chance to thrive again. My job now is to let him ride motorcycles, work out until he's tired, and stay away from the violence he craves. He's an addict and one taste of violence propels him into his glory. One taste is not enough for him, though it's too much for me, and I know that. To move forward and be my own best person, I must deny him while thriving in another venue. I know, down deep, who I am. I'm a cop. Except that I can't be one now. But I am still a sheepdog and I have the greatest admiration for sheepdogs everywhere, and especially for my brothers and sisters in blue. Along the way I showed what I believe to be courage in big situations. Now I work daily to show a different kind — the courage to embrace a new, balanced self.

I still often think about Plutarch's paradox of the wooden ship that leaves port carrying a cargo of new planks and, after springing

leaks along the route, replaces all its planks with ones from its

payload. What is the true nature of a thing that changes along its

journey? Each of us is the same ship all along, and we're all responsible

for ourselves as we change. Though we can't control the storms that

break, thrash, and toss us, we can choose to replace our broken pieces

as we go and become stronger, or we can choose not to and just

capsize.

You can always find reasons to do both.

About the Author

Ryan Garland is medically retired from the Federal Air Marshal Service for post traumatic stress disorder. He is currently pursuing a master's degree in education to become a high school social studies teacher in New Jersey.

Garland graduated from Vanderbilt University in 1996 with a BA in Philosophy. That year, he joined the Metro Nashville Police Department, which awarded him six commendations for life saving, valor, and meritorious service. He also received a Federal Bureau of Investigation award for heroic actions under hostile gunfire.

Garland was selected by the Federal Air Marshal Service in 2001 and spent a great deal of time in Israel under the U.S.

Department of Homeland Security. He was awarded a commendation

for rescue efforts during Hurricane Katrina and several other

distinctions. In 2005, he was assigned to the FBI's Joint Terrorism

Task Force in Newark and engaged in international terrorism

investigations until his retirement in 2009.

He now lives in Kansas City, with his wife, Kristi, and his

German Shepherd, Arya.

Made in the USA
Columbia, SC
30 December 2017